T0304534

THE ROAD OF TRANSITION

THE PATHWAY TO SUCCESSFUL LIVING

Dr. Thaddeus M. Williams Sr.

authorHOUSE®

AuthorHouse™
1663 Liberty Drive
Bloomington, IN 47403
www.authorhouse.com
Phone: 1-800-839-8640

Edited by:
Sarah Bonner, Pensacola, Florida
Kamla Williams, Atlanta, Georgia

Cover Design By:
Taryn Williams, Pensacola, Florida

Website:
www.thewayaheadministries.com

Blogs:
blog.thewayaheadministries.com

First published by AuthorHouse 4/22/2011

ISBN: 978-1-4520-8768-9 (sc)
ISBN: 978-1-4520-8769-6 (e)

Library of Congress Control Number: 2010915746

Printed in the United States of America

Certain stock imagery © Thinkstock.

This book is printed on acid-free paper.

AN EXPLANATION OF ABBREVIATIONS USED IN THE OLD AND NEW TESTAMENTS

The translation used here may be identified by the following code:

Amp – The Amplified New Testament

ASV – The American Standard Version

Bas – The New Testament in Basic English

Con – The Epistles of Paul (W.J. Conybeare)

KJV – The King James Version

Knox – The New Testament in the Translation of Monsignor Ronald Knox

Mof – The New Testament: A New Translation (James Moffatt)

NAB – The New American Bible

NEB – The New English Bible: New Testament

Phi – The New Testament in Modern English (J.B. Phillips)

Tay – Living Letters: The Paraphrased Epistles; Living Gospels: The Paraphrased Gospels; Living Prophecies: The Minor Prophets Paraphrased and Daniel and the Revelation (Kenneth N. Taylor)

TCNT – The Twentieth Century New Testament

TABLE OF CONTENTS

DEDICATION

I dedicate this book to my lovely wife, Vinnie. You have stood by my side since marrying me 25 years ago and your love has stood the test of time. The agape (unconditional love) that we share has endured through some of the toughest times in our lives. Aside from the Word of God, your love has been the springboard for me positioning myself to become a better man, husband and father for God, you, our wonderful children, and the world. My reasons for success begin with God and end with you and that is why I consider myself one of the most blessed men on the planet. *I LOVE YOU, VINNIE!*

- Maurice

INTRODUCTION

Throughout my Christian existence, I have noticed that a large percentage of the Body of Christ has continuously prayed for change and growth. When we begin to pray for change what we are really inviting is transition in our lives. Interestingly, when God begins to answer those prayers for change and growth, many in the faith begin to restrain those prayers and constrain the move of God. I believe that the foregoing argument is confirmation that many are not ready for the move of God as it relates to transitioning.

Any kind of change or modification usually requires something of us. It may require us to give up something or take on some new duty. This demand is what causes people to shrink away from the things of God – because growth and maturity in the things of God is inevitable; however, the fear of the unknown is a much greater yoke. Alternatively, some people pray for change, but intuitively do not believe that God will answer their prayer. Perhaps this stems from their uncertainty and anxiety over the faith needed to believe the promises of God.

There are several biblical examples of God commanding men to change in order to situate themselves for His blessing. In fact, many of those accounts necessitate an act of faith preeminent to the change. Change is diverse and oftentimes, it (change) entails departing from familiar territory to venture into the unchartered regions of our lives and ministry. Many people would have difficulty embracing such newness. However, if serving in any capacity of ministry, this kind of faith is what God requires of us.

There are pastors who believe that change or transition is bad for a church body because there is an inherent fear of losing control. But God didn't call them to control the people; instead He called them to equip the people for the work of the ministry:

> *And he gave some, apostles; and some, prophets; and some, evangelists; and some, pastors and teachers;*

> *For the perfecting of the saints, for the work of the ministry, for the edifying of the body of Christ:*
> *-Ephesians 4:11-12 (KJV)*

> *His "gifts unto men" were varied. Some he made his messengers, some prophets, some preachers of the gospel; to some he gave the power to guide and teach his people.*

> *His gifts were made that Christians might be properly equipped for their service.*
> *-Ephesians 4:11-12 (Phi)*

The purpose of the equipping of the saints is for the various accounts of growth and transition that are an evidentiary result of the Word of God as it is delivered to the believers and non-believers alike. From Genesis chapter 12 and verse 1, when God commanded Abraham to leave his kindred through John chapter 3 and verse 3 when Jesus explained to Nicodemus that a person must be born again to see the Kingdom of God – are examples of the end result when people obey God and follow his plans. In each case we find that there is a blessing attached to obedience and following God's plan for the destiny that He has for each of our lives.

My wife and I have gone through a number of periods of transition in our personal lives as well as members of our local church. Transition demands and requires absolute obedience of a person; and if they are not willing to change, they will be left behind while their leaders and others move on with God.

It has been my observation over a period of several years that people who hear the Word of God and refuse to change or modify their lifestyles or attempt to correct errors that are wrong, will at some point leave the church feeling rejected, out of place, and out of touch – many times mad at the pastor, and set in their way of thinking, whatever it is. Interestingly, their reason for leaving this way is two-fold. For one they want to exercise some control of the pastor (and of the church); and they want their opinion or perspective deemed as a viable option.

Change is a necessary prerequisite to the blessings of the Lord flourishing in our lives. The desire to change should be sparked in our hearts as we receive revelation from God's Word. Because it is the revelation of the Word that gives light and it is the light of the Word that will ultimately produce change in our heart and soul, if we allow it to do so. It is therefore, important to remember that change is good and will keep us from being left behind when it comes to the things of God.

Being a student of the Word of God, I have learned that in order to survive transition a person must have a teachable spirit. They must realize and accept in their hearts that while God is a God of transition – it is a good thing and not a bad thing. The road of transition is an amazingly wonderful road to travel, when understood.

It is my desire that with the help of the Spirit of God – I will share with you some of the things that God has taught me during the transitional times and periods in my life. My prayer for you is that this book (which is inspired by God), will be a help to you in your walk with God and that you will be able to better position yourself for His work and His call!

Further, I pray that you will arrive at a place in your walk wherein you will address transition in your life, not with fear; but with the grace of God, which will allow you to meet the challenges directly – thereby producing growth and maturity. Since transition is a vital part of our walk, I encourage you to have an open heart to what the Spirit of the Lord is speaking through the material contained within these pages. It is my belief that only the strong survive the Road of Transition.

CHAPTER I

Y2K THE NEW MILLENNIUM

I believe that the year 2000 marked the beginning of a transitional period for the Body of Christ. Many feared what was ahead for us as a people as the clock ticked into the new millennium. We are now eleven years into a millennium that many Christians thought they would not live to see.

Webster's Dictionary defines *"millennium"* as *"any period of great happiness, peace, and prosperity."* Based on this definition, it is my belief that the year 2000 was the year that restoration, perfection, and blessing began to manifest in people's lives on a greater level.

TWO DAYS HAVE PASSED

The Word of God informs us that a day is as a thousand years and a thousand years is as one day to the Lord. We know from the Word that Jesus died nearly 2000 years ago to redeem mankind back to God. Before His death, burial, and resurrection Jesus told the Jews that he would raise the temple up in three days. They thought that He was speaking of a natural temple, but He was speaking of Himself. Jesus was saying that when they crucified Him, He would be resurrected in three days:

...That with the Lord a day counts as a thousand years and a thousand years count as a day.

-II Peter 3:8 (Knox)

Jesus answered and said unto them, Destroy this temple, and in three days I will raise it up.

Then said the Jews, Forty and six years was this temple in building, and wilt thou rear it up in three days?

But he spake of the temple of his body.

-John 2:19-21 (KJV)

I believe that the above scriptures have a prophetic meaning that relates to the Body of Christ today. Allow me to explain – In the book of John 2:19, Jesus said that the temple would be raised on the third day. First Corinthians 6:19 and 12:27 states that we are the temple of God and the Body of Christ. In reading 2 Peter 3:8 we know that 2,000 years is the equivalent to two days since 1,000 years equals one day to the Lord.

What? know ye not that your body is the temple of the Holy Ghost which is in you, which ye have of God, and ye are not your own?

-1 Corinthians 6:19 (KJV)

Now you [collectively] are Christ's body and [individually] you are members of it, each part severally and distinct [each with his own place and function].

-1 Corinthians 12:27 (Amp)

We should note that two days have passed since Jesus' death, burial, and resurrection. Therefore, I believe that the year 2000 marked the beginning of God transitioning His people into a position to receive the fullness of what He has for His people in these last days. Moreover, the year 2000 was the beginning of the third day - the day of resurrection; and it is during this time that the Church began to flow in a more intense way because of the "revitalization" power that came upon her (the church). The same power that raised Christ from the dead has begun to manifest itself in a greater level because the Church has greater works to do than our Lord and Savior, Jesus Christ.

Verily, verily, I say unto you, He that believeth on me, the works that I do shall he do also; and greater works than these shall he do; because I go unto my Father.

-John 14:12 (KJV)

ON THE THIRD DAY

When reading the Bible, we find that a great deal took place on the third day throughout Jesus' ministry on earth. For example, in Luke Chapter 13 and verse 32, Jesus said that He would be perfected on the third day. In this verse of scripture the word "perfected" means "to be complete or to be made complete." So Jesus was saying that on the third day He would have accomplished everything God, the Father sent Him to do.

Chiefly, his mission was to redeem mankind. Because of Jesus, mankind will no longer have to stay in the place where he fell when Adam gave everything away in the garden. Why? Because now we are complete, or made perfect, through Christ Jesus and we were raised from the dead with Him. Therefore, if He was perfected on the third day, then so were we. In other words, the Lord has perfected that which concerns us:

And ye are complete in him, which is the head of all principality and power:

-Colossians 2:10 (KJV)

… and in Christ Jesus He raised us up with Him from the dead, and seated us with Him in the heavens.

-Ephesians 2:6 (Con)

The LORD will perfect that which concerneth me: thy mercy, O LORD, endureth forever: forsake not the works of thine own hands.

-Psalm 138:8 (KJV)

I believe the new millennium marked the beginning of a dispensation of great happiness, peace, and prosperity for the Church body. However, (sadly), many will not experience the blessings of this season because they fear making the necessary transition that will eventually challenge them to change their attitude. A person's mindset must be changed by the Word of God before he/she can receive the aforementioned blessings for themselves.

CHAPTER II

TRANSITION DEFINED

Webster's Dictionary defines "transition," is "a passing from one condition, form, stage, activity, place, etc. to another." The word "change" as "to cause to become different; alter; transform; convert." So we may conclude that "change" is the prerequisite for "transition." Therefore, one must be willing to change in order to make the transition into the way God is doing things in these last days. God is doing a new thing in the earth today. The way in which we have grown to have organized religion is quickly becoming a thing of the past and God is now setting things back in order – the way He intended them to be:

> *But forget all that it is nothing compared to what I'm going to do.*
> *For I'm going to do a brand new thing. See I have already begun!*
> *Don't you see it?*
> **-Isaiah 43:18-19 (Tay)**

It is not my intention to declare that God is changing the way He has always done things. Absolutely not! God never changes in the sense of "Oh I guess I was wrong – better go to Plan B". That is not the way that God operates. He is a God of law and order and the way He plans it is the way that it goes!

> *...who is himself never subject to change.*
> **-James 1:17 (TCT)**

The Church is beginning to live by faith as God originally planned. Such living allows the Lord God an avenue wherein He can move on our behalf. By contrast, in times past, the Church as a whole has been full of doubt and unbelief, therefore, God could do few miracles among us.

> *And he did not many works of power there, because of their unbelief (their lack of faith in the divine mission of Jesus.)*
> **-Matthew 13:58 (Amp)**

The flow of God's miracle-working power isn't anything new. But in a sense, it is new to the Church because we are just starting to transition over into the realm of faith in full capacity. Simply, the Body of Christ is beginning to live and move in the realm of miracles, signs, and wonders – a realm that has always existed since the beginning of time. It is the realm where God lives and operates. It is the realm of faith and glory or the realm of the supernatural.

> *Now the just shall live by faith…*
> **-Hebrews 10:38 (KJV)**

Spiritually speaking, you and I live in the realm that influences the natural realm. The Bible tells us that we are seated together with Christ in the heavenly places, or the realm of faith. In other words, we are in the world, but we are not of the world.

> *And hath raised us up together, and made us sit together in heavenly places in Christ Jesus:*
> **-Ephesians 2:6 (KJV)**

> *…and has lifted us right out of the old life to take our place with Him in Christ Jesus in the Heavens.*
> **-Ephesians 2:6 (Phi)**

> *I have given them thy word; and the world hath hated them, because they are not of the world, even as I am not of the world.*

> *I pray not that thou shouldest take them out of the world, but that thou shouldest keep them from the evil.*

They are not of the world, even as I am not of the world.
-John 17:14-16 (KJV)

Remember that "transition" is defined as "a passing from one condition, form, stage, activity, place, etc. to another." As I mentioned earlier, when Adam fell in the garden, a transition took place. Mankind fell from a place of life and prosperity to a place of death and poverty. God at the beginning of the new millennium, (2000 – which marked the beginning of the third day) began to raise His body up and is restoring it back to the place of great happiness, peace, and prosperity.

WHY CHANGE?

Earlier we defined change as "to cause to become different; alter; transform; convert." Change is the prerequisite for transition and both are necessary for reaching your destiny. However, this process of change and transition leaves most believers frustrated and for many becomes a permanent roadblock. My friend, if you are not willing to change for the better, then you are not going to grow, which means you will never reach your full potential in God.

So how does change occur in one's life? That's a very good question, and I have the answer for you. Change occurs when you allow your mind to be renewed by God's Word (Romans 12:1-2). In other words, the constant intake of God's Word produces manifested change in one's mindset. Please understand that the renewing of one's mind is an ongoing process, which takes place by applying the Word of God to our souls through reading and meditating. However, don't make the mistake of thinking that acquiring more knowledge means your mind is being renewed. Knowledge without application is powerless in promoting change. It takes the Word of God, and you not responding in the same manner to old temptations. It's only when our minds are renewed that we are able to prove what the acceptable and perfect will of God is and resist temptations that have once held us captive. The Word is the only thing that has the power to penetrate the hardness of a person's heart (Hebrews 4:12), and in order to allow the Word to go deep into our spirits, we must present our spirits, souls and bodies to God as a living sacrifice. This commitment on our part will signify to him that we are willing to decrease [refrain from being carnally minded] so that he might increase in our lives.

'CHANGE' THE OFFSPRING OF SPIRITUAL GROWTH

It is the desire of every Christian to arrive at the destination the Lord has called them to. To get there will require the believer to grow in the understanding, wisdom, and knowledge of the Word of God. The late *John F. Kennedy said: "Change is the law of life. And those who look only to the past or present are certain to miss the future."* Simply put, failing to change your mindset will cause you to miss what God has planned for your future! It's when you make up your mind to grow spiritually through His Word, that you will notice an undeniable change in your reactions, mindset and the decisions you make. Absolute [genuine] change is the fruit of spiritual growth and advancement in the Word of God. If you aren't noticing change in your life, it is because you've become stagnant [motionless, sluggish, immobile, dormant or inactive] in your spiritual growth. To obtain different results, you must decide to do things differently, starting with changing your mindset.

Below are three things that will assist you in your spiritual growth; 1) start to discipline yourself in the Word. This will begin the process of changing your mindset. 2) Change the way you pray and become more consistent in your prayer life. This will strengthen your inner man and prepare you for what's ahead in God and 3) Set new boundaries for yourself; refuse to indulge in immoral activities because bad habits contaminate your spirit, soul [your mind, will and emotions] and body.

Remember that growth produces change, and change manifest when you apply and work the principles of God's Word in your life. Please understand, *change is the offspring of spiritual growth* and it will never occur as a result of your ability and will power. You must decide that you want to change, and by the power of God you can. Therefore, take the required steps to grow and mature in your relationship with the Lord. He is there to help you.

THE 7H'S TO CHANGE

Allowing the Word to change our mindset doesn't happen overnight. This is where so many people miss God, they want fast results, but it takes time before you see the fruit of a seed. Not only do people want overnight change, some just flat out refuse to change because it will require action on their part. *LAZINESS* is one of seven hindrances (7H's) to change in a person mindset. The other six are **PRIDE, REBELLION, FEAR, DISTRACTION, DECEPTION** and **IGNORANCE**. Let's examine each of them below to see how they will affect a person's life if not dealt with properly.

THE CAUSE (C) AND AFFECT (A)

(C) **LAZINESS:** "I don't feel like changing."
(A) Laziness will lead to a person's poverty. So don't expect to succeed if you are too lazy to study and act on the Word of God.

> *How long wilt thou sleep, O sluggard? when wilt thou arise out of thy sleep?*
>
> *Yet a little sleep, a little slumber, a little folding of the hands to sleep:*
>
> *So shall thy poverty come as one that travelleth, and thy want as an armed man.*
> *- Proverbs 6:9-11 (KJV)*

(C) **PRIDE:** "I don't need to change."
(A) Pride and arrogance always precede destruction and a fall. Pride will separate you from the presence of God. It did Lucifer (Isaiah 14:12-13).

> *Pride goeth before destruction, and an haughty spirit before a fall.*
> *- Proverbs 16:18 (KJV)*

(C) **REBELLION:** "I don't want to change"
(A) Rebellion will cost you your authority (kingship), your power to rule and reign (anointing) and Gods perfect will for your life (destiny). Because Saul disobeyed God, he lost everything he had as king.

> *Samuel also said unto Saul, The LORD sent me to anoint thee to be king over his people, over Israel: now therefore hearken thou unto the voice of the words of the LORD.*

Thus saith the LORD of hosts, I remember that which Amalek did to Israel, how he laid wait for him in the way, when he came up from Egypt.

Now go and smite Amalek, and utterly destroy all that they have, and spare them not; but slay both man and woman, infant and suckling, ox and sheep, camel and ass.

And Saul gathered the people together, and numbered them in Telaim, two hundred thousand footmen, and ten thousand men of Judah.

And Saul came to a city of Amalek, and laid wait in the valley.

And Saul said unto the Kenites, Go, depart, get you down from among the Amalekites, lest I destroy you with them: for ye shewed kindness to all the children of Israel, when they came up out of Egypt. So the Kenites departed from among the Amalekites.

And Saul smote the Amalekites from Havilah until thou comest to Shur, that is over against Egypt.

And he took Agag the king of the Amalekites alive, and utterly destroyed all the people with the edge of the sword.

But Saul and the people spared Agag, and the best of the sheep, and of the oxen, and of the fatlings, and the lambs, and all that was good, and would not utterly destroy them: but every thing that was vile and refuse, that they destroyed utterly.

And Samuel said, Hath the LORD as great delight in burnt offerings and sacrifices, as in obeying the voice of the LORD? Behold, to obey is better than sacrifice, and to hearken than the fat of rams.

For rebellion is as the sin of witchcraft, and stubbornness is as iniquity and idolatry. Because thou hast rejected the word of the LORD, he hath also rejected thee from being king.

- *1 Samuel 15:1-9 and 22-23 (KJV)*

(C) **DISTRACTION:** "I can't stay focused"
(A) Focusing on your circumstances verses God's Word will hinder you from becoming all that God has called you to be. Peter was hindered in his ability to walk on water when he began to focus on the wind [storm] and not on what Jesus (God) had empowered him to do.

> *And Peter answered him and said, Lord, if it be thou, bid me come unto thee on the water.*
>
> *And he said, Come. And when Peter was come down out of the ship, he walked on the water, to go to Jesus.*
>
> *But when he saw the wind boisterous, he was afraid; and beginning to sink, he cried, saying, Lord, save me.*
> *- Matthew 14:28-30 (KJV)*

(C) **FEAR:** "I'm afraid to change"
(A) Where fear is present so is torment. Fear produces the results of the enemy just as faith produces the results of God in your life.

> *But Jesus, on hearing this, answered him, Do not be seized with alarm or struck with fear; simply believe [in Me as able to do this], and she shall be made well.*
> *- Luke 8:50 (Amp)*

(C) **DECEPTION:** "I can make it on my own"
(A) Trusting in your own ability, limits your productivity. It bends the truth, produces false hope and makes you lord and savior [god] of your life.

> *Thou shalt have none other gods before me.*
> *- Deuteronomy 5:7 (KJV)*
>
> *Trust in the LORD with all your heart; do not depend on your own understanding.*
>
> *Seek His will in all you do, and He will show you which path to take.*

> *Don't be impressed with your own wisdom. Instead, fear the LORD and turn away from evil.*
>
> **- Proverbs 3:5-7 NLT**

(C) **IGNORANCE**: "I've never thought about changing."
(A) Ignorance will cost you your right to stand in the presence of God and forfeit your children inheritance in God.

> *My people are ruined because they don't know what's right or true. Because you've turned your back on knowledge, I've turned my back on you priests. Because you refuse to recognize the revelation of God, I'm no longer recognizing your children.*
>
> **- Hosea 4:6 (MSG)**

Locating the above hindrances in your life and committing to getting rid of them will put you on the path to change. Therefore, I encourage you to keep the faith and allow the Word to work in your life.

CHAPTER III

BIBLICAL ACCOUNTS OF TRANSITION

The Bible gives various accounts of God transitioning His people to a place of blessings and He is still doing it today. He is restoring everything to its original state. Many do not realize that *transition* is a sign of growth and maturity. Remember, "transition" means to pass from one state to another and God wants to take His people from glory to glory to prosper them. Therefore, we can say that transition is also a sign of prosperity and promotion. The Word of God states that Jesus came to seek and save that which was lost. He came to seek and save those who had fallen from their original place of authority and power.

And all of us, as with unveiled face, [because we] continued to behold [in the Word of God] as in a mirror the glory of the Lord, are constantly being transfigured into His very own image in ever increasing splendor and from one degree of glory to another; [for this comes] from the Lord [Who is] the Spirit.
-II Corinthians 3:18 (Amp)

For the Son of man is come to seek and to save that which was lost.
-Luke 19:10 (KJV)

Although mankind was lost and separated from God when Adam fell in the garden, God sent His Son to redeem man back to himself; Being redeemed or coming back to that first place puts [man] in a position of great happiness, peace, and prosperity:

And they sung a new song, saying, Thou art worthy to take the book, and to open the seals thereof: for thou wast slain, and hast redeemed us to God by thy blood out of every kindred, and tongue, and people, and nation...

-Revelation 5:9 (KJV)

The reason that it was necessary for our redemption is because we needed a path to connect again with the Father with whom we had lost connection. Man was created to prosper and have dominion in the earth, but Satan received our promise through Adam's fall. The enmity that existed between mankind and God could only be obliterated with a pure sacrifice. Mankind fell from its place of authority to a place of slavery, from life to death. In other words, a spiritual transition took place and God's creation, "Man," the one that was created in the image of God fell from the place of great happiness, peace, prosperity, and dominion to the place of sadness, pain, torment, worry, bondage, and poverty. But glory to God we have been redeemed!

And God said, Let us make man in our image, after our likeness: and let them have dominion over the fish of the sea, and over the fowl of the air, and over the cattle, and over all the earth, and over every creeping thing that creepeth upon the earth.

-Genesis 1:26 (KJV)

Christ hath redeemed us from the curse of the law, being made a curse for us: for it is written, Cursed is every one that hangeth on a tree:

-Galatians 3:13 (KJV)

Earlier I mentioned that there are various examples in the Word of God that illustrates God transitioning His people to a place of blessing. Let's start with Exodus 3:7-10, where God sent Moses to Pharaoh to command him to let the people of God go. Keep in mind as you read the below passage of scriptures that Moses is a type of Christ, Pharaoh is a type of the devil, Egypt represents the place of bondage, and Israel is a type of the Church – God's chosen people.

And the LORD said, I have surely seen the affliction of my people which are in Egypt, and have heard their cry by reason of their taskmasters; for I know their sorrows;

And I am come down to deliver them out of the hand of the Egyptians, and to bring them up out of that land unto a good land and a large, unto a land flowing with milk and honey; unto the place of the Canaanites, and the Hittites, and the Amorites, and the Perizzites, and the Hivites, and the Jebusites.

Now therefore, behold, the cry of the children of Israel is come unto me: and I have also seen the oppression wherewith the Egyptians oppress them.

Come now therefore, and I will send thee unto Pharaoh, that thou mayest bring forth my people the children of Israel out of Egypt.
-Exodus 3:7-10 (KJV)

Prior to Israel's captivity, God made a covenant with Abraham. God made Abraham the father of many nations and gave him the land of Canaan – the land that flowed with milk and honey before he left his home country.

So Abram departed, as the LORD had spoken unto him; and Lot went with him: and Abram was seventy and five years old when he departed out of Haran.

And Abram took Sarai his wife, and Lot his brother's son, and all their substance that they had gathered, and the souls that they had gotten in Haran; and they went forth to go into the land of Canaan; and into the land of Canaan they came.

And Abram passed through the land unto the place of Sichem, unto the plain of Moreh. And the Canaanite was then in the land.

And the LORD appeared unto Abram, and said, Unto thy seed will I give this land: and there builded he an altar unto the LORD, who appeared unto him.

-Genesis 12:4-7 (KJV)

Thou art the LORD the God, who didst choose Abram, and broughtest him forth out of Ur of the Chaldees, and gavest him the name of Abraham;

And foundest his heart faithful before thee, and madest a covenant with him to give the land of the Canaanites, the Hittites, the Amorites, and the Perizzites, and the Jebusites, and the Girgashites, to give it, I say, to his seed, and hast performed thy words; for thou art righteous:

-Nehemiah 9:7-8 (KJV)

And Abram was very rich in cattle, in silver, and in gold.

-Genesis 13:2 (KJV)

However, before Abraham could receive the blessing of the covenant, he had to make a transition. Abraham had to get out of his comfort zone and trust God. In other words, Abraham was challenged to leave his home country, family, and friends to receive what God had in store for him. He had to make up his mind to follow God into a strange land – a place that was unfamiliar to him and his family. Because Abraham obeyed the word of the Lord, he found favor with God and was called "faithful" and his obedience to God's command was imputed unto him for righteousness.

[Urged on] by faith Abraham, when he was called, obeyed and went forth to a place which he was destined to receive as an inheritance; and he went, although he did not know or trouble his mind about where he was to go.

[Prompted] by faith he dwelt as a temporary resident in the land which was designated in the promise [of God, though he was like a stranger] in a strange country, living in tents with Isaac and Jacob, fellow heirs with him of the same promise.

-Hebrews 11:8-9 (Amp)

So then they which be of faith are blessed with faithful Abraham.
-Galatians 3:9 (KJV)

And the scripture was fulfilled which saith, Abraham believed God, and it was imputed unto him for righteousness: and he was called the Friend of God.
-James 2:23 (KJV)

Looking at Hebrews 11:8, we see that it was destined for Abraham to receive for an inheritance — the land that God had promised to him and his seed. But it was up to him to make the transition from his old lifestyle to the lifestyle God had in store for him. Abraham had to be willing to accept change. It is the same with the Church as a whole. God is prompting the Church to move or transition into the place that He has given us as an inheritance. But many are looking at the promises of God through doubt and unbelief. Therefore, they are unable to enter into their inheritance.

The Bible tells us that Abraham staggered not at the promise of God through unbelief but was fully persuaded that God would do what He had promised.

Who against hope believed in hope, that he might become the father of many nations, according to that which was spoken, so shall thy seed be.

And being not weak in faith, he considered not his own body now dead, when he was about an hundred years old, neither yet the deadness of Sara's womb:

He staggered not at the promise of God through unbelief; but was strong in faith, giving glory to God;

And being fully persuaded that, what he had promised, he was able also to perform.

And therefore it was imputed to him for righteousness.
-Romans 4:18-22 (KJV)

Just like Abraham you and I should take God at His Word and move or make the transition He has called us to make. Even if the place is a strange land, we should know in our hearts that God is faithful and that He is leading us to our land that flows with milk and honey.

The promise was made to Abraham and his seed. Somewhere between the promise being given and the people of God entering into the land of promise, they became slaves to Pharaoh:

Now there arose up a new king over Egypt, which knew not Joseph.

And he said unto his people, Behold, the people of the children of Israel are more and mightier than we:

Come on, let us deal wisely with them; lest they multiply, and it come to pass, that, when there falleth out any war, they join also unto our enemies, and fight against us, and so get them up out of the land.

Therefore they did set over them taskmasters to afflict them with their burdens. And they built for Pharaoh treasure cities, Pithom and Raamses.

But the more they afflicted them, the more they multiplied and grew. And they were grieved because of the children of Israel.

And the Egyptians made the children of Israel to serve with rigour:

And they made their lives bitter with hard bondage, in morter, and in brick, and in all manner of service in the field: all their service, wherein they made them serve, was with rigour.
                                                              -Exodus 1:8-14 (KJV)

But God remembered His covenant with Abraham, their father. So he sent them a redeemer to lead them out of bondage and to the land that He had promised Abraham, which was the land of great happiness, peace, and prosperity.

And God heard their groaning, and God remembered his covenant with Abraham, with Isaac, and with Jacob.

And God looked upon the children of Israel, and God had respect unto them.
                                                              -Exodus 2:24-25 (KJV)

MENTAL SLAVERY

The children of God were held in bondage for many years before entering the promise land. They became accustomed to the way they were treated and the way they lived. Complacent in their thinking, they became mentally enslaved. Slavery became their comfort zone because they had forgotten the promise God made to Abraham. God sent Moses to lead His people out of bondage. During their exile from Egypt, the once-enslaved Jews had to travel to the promise land by way of the wilderness. This was the road of transition for them. It was during this wilderness experience that the children of Israel had to learn to fully trust and believe God.

After their release from Egypt, Pharaoh's heart was hardened and he pursued the people of God in great anger. The pressure of Pharaoh's pursuit was so great on the children of Israel they began to murmur and complain. They all became cowards at heart, for fear of Pharaoh. They were so afraid that they were willing to give up their freedom and inheritance to serve Pharaoh and his people once again.

And when Pharaoh drew nigh, the children of Israel lifted up their eyes, and, behold, the Egyptians marched after them; and they were sore afraid: and the children of Israel cried out unto the LORD.

And they said unto Moses, Because there were no graves in Egypt, hast thou taken us away to die in the wilderness? Wherefore hast thou dealt thus with us, to carry us forth out of Egypt?

Is not this the word that we did tell thee in Egypt, saying, Let us alone, that we may serve the Egyptians? For it had been better for us to serve the Egyptians, than that we should die in the wilderness.

And Moses said unto the people, Fear ye not, standstill, and see the salvation of the LORD, which he will shew to you today: for the Egyptians whom ye have seen today, ye shall see them again no more for ever.

-Exodus 14:10-13 (KJV)

Let us pause a moment and examine the above passage of scripture as it relates to us today. Remember that Moses is a type of Christ, Pharaoh is a type of the devil, and the children of Israel represent the Church. In light of that, verse 10 of Exodus 14 says that as the devil (Pharaoh) drew near to the Church (Israel) they became fearful to the point that they thought that Moses (Christ) had lead them out in the desert (an uncultivated region without inhabitants) to die. My friend, today the desert might represent the place where you are standing believing God for your unsaved loved one, or for your healing. Which brings me to a very important point: When we as children of God choose to make the transitions that God requires us to make, at some point we may feel like we are all alone or in the middle of nowhere (the wilderness)? Why? Because spiritually speaking we have ventured into unfamiliar territory, a region that we are not accustomed to.

It is during these times that it appears that the devil is on our trail in high pursuit to keep us from receiving—or should I say, entering into—our inheritance. Many times, just as the children of Israel, we begin to murmur and complain and for some unknown reason we begin to think that we would have been better off staying where we were and choosing not to obey God. But we should always take the advice Moses gave the people of God in the 13th verse of Exodus 14. We should fear not, standstill, and see the salvation of the Lord.

MOSES TO JOSHUA

Although the promise was made to Abraham and his seed, Abraham did not enter the promise land, but was allowed by God only to see it from afar before his death. His death did not cause God to go back on His Word.

> *By faith Abraham, when he was called to go out into a place which he should after receive for an inheritance, obeyed; and he went out, not knowing whither he went.*

> *By faith he sojourned in the land of promise, as in a strange country, dwelling in tabernacles with Isaac and Jacob, the heirs with him of the same promise:*

> *For he looked for a city which hath foundations, whose builder and maker is God.*

These all [including Abraham] died in faith, not having received the promises, but having seen them afar off, and were persuaded of them, and embraced them, and confessed that they were strangers and pilgrims on the earth.

-Hebrews 11:8-10 & 13 (KJV)

After Abraham's death, God raised up another leader to lead His people to the place of promise. That leader was Moses, the one who brought the Israelites out of slavery and led them to the promise land. The promise represented prosperity, peace, and joy and God wanted the best for His people. But in order for them to get what God had for them, they had to make a change. They had to leave the old in order to receive the new; leave slavery to enter into liberty; leave lack to receive abundance. Unfortunately, many did not receive or enter into what God had for them because of doubt and unbelief.

While it is said, Today if ye will hear his voice, harden not your hearts, as in the provocation.

For some, when they had heard, did provoke howbeit not all that came out of Egypt by Moses.

But with whom was he grieved forty years? Was it not with them that had sinned, whose carcases fell in the wilderness?

And to whom sware he that they should not enter into his rest, but to them that believed not?

So we see that they could not enter in because of unbelief.

-Hebrews 3:15-19 (KJV)

God's people had been enslaved for many years and God heard their cry and delivered them from their sorrows and pain. He had prepared a place of rest for them but many died on the road of transition, never reaching or even seeing the land of promise or their place of rest.

Remember the word which Moses the servant of the LORD commanded you, saying, The LORD your God hath given you rest, and hath given you this land.

-Joshua 1:13 (KJV)

For the children of Israel walked forty years in the wilderness, till all the people that were men of war, which came out of Egypt, were consumed, because they obeyed not the voice of the LORD: unto whom the LORD sware that he would not shew them the land, which the LORD sware unto their fathers that he would give us, a land that floweth with milk and honey.

-Joshua 5:6 (KJV)

Even though some of the people Moses led out of Egypt died in the wilderness, and Moses himself was not permitted to enter in, God gave Moses the opportunity to see the land. Then at the age of 120 Moses died in the land of Moab.

And the LORD said unto him, This is the land which I sware unto Abraham, unto Isaac, and unto Jacob, saying, I will give it unto thy seed: I have caused thee to see it with thine eyes, but thou shalt not go over thither.

So Moses the servant of the LORD died there in the land of Moab, according to the word of the LORD.

-Deuteronomy 34:4-5 (KJV)

But Moses' death didn't stop God from moving on His people's behalf. God still aimed to fulfill the covenant He made with Abraham. His mission was to get His people into their place of rest and peace because the covenant was sealed by His Name.

For when God made promise to Abraham, because he could swear by no greater, he sware by himself,

Saying, Surely blessing I will bless thee, and multiplying I will multiply thee.

-Hebrews 6:13-14 (KJV)

Remember that we are talking about transition and I am trying to help you understand that when God commands you to change it's because He is working to get you into your place of blessing, your Garden of Eden. You and I have a destiny in God and our destiny is our place of blessing and the land that God has promised us.

Transferring the Vision

Before Moses died in the Land of Moab, the Word tells us that he laid hands on Joshua, the son of Nun. Joshua was to lead God's people into the promise land. He was the successor and minister of Moses and the leader of a new generation of people, a generation of warriors, giant killers, and city takers.

And Joshua the son of Nun was full of the spirit of wisdom; for Moses had laid his hands upon him: and the children of Israel hearkened unto him, and did as the LORD commanded Moses.

-Deuteronomy 34:9 (KJV)

Now after the death of Moses the servant of the LORD it came to pass, that the LORD spake unto Joshua the son of Nun, Moses' minister, saying,

Moses my servant is dead; now therefore arise, go over this Jordan, thou, and all this people, unto the land which I do give to them, even to the children of Israel.

-Joshua 1:1-2 (KJV)

When Moses laid hands on Joshua, I believe the vision of God was imparted to the leader of this new breed of people. In other words, a spiritual transition took place and the old way of doing things came to an end. It was going to take a different type of leader to get the people into the land of promise. Notice I said *"into"* the land of promise.

Moses was a shepherd and God used him to gather His flock to lead them out of the land of bondage *"to"* the place that He had promised them. Joshua, on the other hand, was a warrior, a man of strength, faith, and power and God used him to take the people *"into"* the land. In other words, he was the possessor of the land that God had promised.

Possessing the Land

Joshua was a strong and courageous man who knew in his heart what God had promised and nothing was going to stop him from receiving his blessing. He didn't see himself as a "grasshopper" as some did; he saw only the promise of God.

And there we saw the giants, the sons of Anak, which come of the giants: and we were in our own sight as grasshoppers, and so we were in their sight.

-Numbers 13:33 (KJV)

Joshua was faithful and obedient to the voice of the Lord and because of that God caused his enemies to flee seven ways. His enemies feared him because they knew God was with him and the children of Israel ate the fruit of the Land of Canaan that year. The land that God promised Abraham and his seed was possessed and occupied by His people. Why? Because God is a covenant-keeper and not a covenant-breaker.

And it came to pass, when all the kings of the Amorites, which were on the side of Jordan westward, and all the kings of the Canaanites, which were by the sea, heard that the LORD had dried up the waters of Jordan from before the children of Israel, until we were passed over, that their heart melted, neither was there spirit in them anymore, because of the children of Israel.

And the manna ceased on the morrow after they had eaten of the old corn of the land; neither had the children of Israel manna anymore; but they did eat of the fruit of the land of Canaan that year.

-Joshua 5:1 and 12 (KJV)

With the above in mind I would like to make this point: Many times while going through transition, we begin to see ourselves in a distorted way. We think less of ourselves and forget that we have a covenant with God. But we should be like Joshua and keep our eyes on the promise and possess our land. No matter what giants are in our way we should remember that the battle is won and the giants are defeated. They were defeated by our Lord and Savior Jesus Christ. Praise God we have the victory in the Name of Jesus! Therefore, possess your land of promise because it belongs to you!

CHAPTER IV

THE TRANSITIONING
OF THE CHURCH

Years ago God told a man of God something concerning the Body of Christ. God told him that the next move of God would be Him [God] moving His people. You see, for years the Church has been waiting on God to move. But God has been waiting on His people to realize who they are and what they have in Him. Living in darkness, doubt, and unbelief for years the Church has been robbed of her power and strength. But something great has happened in the Body of Christ. God is pouring out of His Spirit on all flesh in these last days. So what am I saying? I am saying that the Church is beginning to stir herself up in the Holy Ghost and flow in the things of God.

This I say therefore, and testify in the Lord, that ye henceforth walk not as other Gentiles walk, in the vanity of their mind,

Having the understanding darkened, being alienated from the life of God through the ignorance that is in them, because of the blindness of their heart:

-Ephesians 4:17-18 (KJV)

So this I say and solemnly testify in [the name of] the Lord [as in His presence], that you must no longer live as the heathen (the Gentiles) do in their perverseness [in the folly, vanity, and emptiness of their souls and the futility] of their minds.

Their moral understanding is darkened and their reasoning is beclouded. [They are] alienated (estrange, self-banished) from the life of God [with no share in it; this is] because of the ignorance (the want of knowledge and perception, the willful blindness)that is deep-seated in them, due to their hardness of heart [to the insensitiveness of their moral natural].

-Ephesians 4:17-18 (Amp)

...They live blindfold

-Ephesians 4:18 (Phi)

Seeing therefore, it remaineth that some must enter therein, and they to whom it was first preached entered not in because of unbelief:

-Hebrews 4:6 (KJV)

And it shall come to pass in the last days, saith God, I will pour out of my Spirit upon all flesh: and your sons and your daughters shall prophesy, and your young men shall see visions, and your old men shall dream dreams:

-Acts 2:17 (KJV)

Wherefore I put thee in remembrance that thou stir up the gift of God, which is in thee by the putting on of my hands.

-II Timothy 1:6 (KJV)

But ye, beloved, building up yourselves on your most holy faith, praying in the Holy Ghost,

-Jude 20 (KJV)

Saint of God, there is a refreshing flow of the Spirit of God moving throughout His body. Notice I said a refreshing flow of the Spirit of God *"is"* moving throughout the Body of Christ. That means that it is happening now! Not "going to happen" but this move of God is taking place even as you read this book. God is reviving His Church and the Church is beginning to live in the light and life of the Word of God.

In the beginning was the Word and the Word was with God, and the Word was God.

The same was in the beginning with God.

All things were made by him and without him was not anything made that was made.

In him was life; and the life was the light of men.
-John 1:1-4 (KJV)

It is the spirit that quickeneth; the flesh profiteth nothing: the words that I speak unto you, they are spirit and they are life
-John 6:63 (KJV)

But if the Spirit of him that raised up Jesus from the dead dwell in you, he that raised up Christ from the dead shall also quicken your mortal bodies by his Spirit that dwelleth in you
-Romans 8:11 (KJV)

The light I am referring to is the revelation of God's Word and the life is the life of Jesus that now resides in our inner man. This life is the product of studying the Word of God until it penetrates our entire being. Once this Word is in our hearts, then the Spirit of God will illuminate it to bring forth revelation. Therefore, life is the product of revelation.

The Transition of the Local Church

Pastors throughout the country are starting to feed their flocks the Word of God instead of religion or the enticing words of man's wisdom (1 Corinthians 2:4). Churches around the world are rising up and taking over their cities, countries, and states because the people of God have realized the power and authority they have in Christ Jesus. Nations are being taken by force for Christ because the Body of Christ has awakened out of its sleep. Vision and direction are being imparted to the Church because the unadulterated truth is being preached and taught from pulpits around the world. Pastors are no longer compromising the Word of God for fear of people leaving their congregations. They are allowing the Spirit of God to move and have liberty in the midst of them. Revelation knowledge has come to the people of God.

THE CALL HAS NO GENDER OR COLOR

Lie not one to another, seeing that ye have put off the old man with his deeds;

And have put on the new man, which is renewed in knowledge after the image of him that created him:

Where there is neither Greek nor Jew, circumcision nor uncircumcision, Barbarian, Scythian, bond nor free: but Christ is all, and in all.

-Colossians 3:9-11 (KJV)

And saw heaven opened, and a certain vessel descending unto him, as it had been a great sheet knit at the four corners, and let down to the earth:

Wherein were all manner of four-footed beasts of the earth, and wild beasts, and creeping things, and fowls of the air.

And there came a voice to him, Rise, Peter; kill, and eat.

But Peter said, Not so, Lord; for I have never eaten anything that is common or unclean.

And the voice spake unto him again the second time, What God hath cleansed, that call not thou common.

This was done thrice: and the vessel was received up again into heaven.

And he said unto them, Ye know how that it is an unlawful thing for a man that is a Jew to keep company, or come unto one of another nation; but God hath shewed me that I should not call any man common or unclean

-Acts 10:11-16 and 28 (KJV)

Over the years I have come to realize that the call of God has no gender or color. If God does not see male or female, or black or white when it comes to the call, then why does the Church? The Bible tells us that God has no respect of persons. So if God is not racist or prejudiced when it comes to the call, then why does prejudice and racism exist in some churchs today?

During my childhood I attended an African Methodist Episcopal (AME) church that was located in a poor section of Birmingham, Alabama. During those days the white families had their own churches and the black families had theirs in a different part of town. For years while I was growing up, I wondered why there were never any white families in our church. Being so young I could never figure it out, but I knew that what I was seeing was wrong, both in my sight and in God's.

Thank God that this practice now only exists in pockets of society and cities and that racism and separatism is not as prominent as it once was. In fact multicultural churches and congregations exist in every city and are an integral part of society. The preaching of the truth of the Word of God has helped to facilitate this situation.

THE GENDER ISSUE

Along with the many racial questions that were on my mind as a child, I often wondered and never understood why all the preachers were men. My grandmother was a minister, but she was the only woman I ever saw preach from a pulpit. Now I must admit that there were more women that attended church than men in those days, but none of them were preachers. These women mostly sat in one section of the building called the "Amen Corner." They wore white hats and dresses and they looked like they were going to work in a hospital rather than attend church. These ladies' responsibility was to take care of the other women who got what we called back then "happy." Getting happy in a black church meant that a person—and most of the time it was a woman—would get touched during the preaching of the message or singing. They would shake violently, sometimes to the point of losing their wigs, while having what I call a religious fit. In other words, they would freak out even if a dead sermon was preached or the music was unanointed. But thank God those days are over. That's right; the days of racism and women keeping silent in the church are over. Certainly, there is a very small percentage of churches that still operate according to the old rules of man. (Notice I said "man" and not "God.") Overall, things are changing in the Body of Christ. Transition has taken place in the realm of the Spirit and all the walls of racial strife and prejudice are beginning to come down; and the women are beginning to preach the Word around the world. Women, such as my wife Vinnie Williams, Joyce Meyer, Gloria Copeland, and Taffi Dollar are just a few women who have taken their place in the Body of Christ as leading ministers of the Word and power of God. These and many others like them are no longer hindered by the doctrines of men, and I thank the Lord for them.

> *Let your women keep silence in the churches: for it is not permitted unto them to speak; but they are commanded to be under obedience, as also saith the law*
>
> **-I Corinthians 14:34 (KJV)**

For years the above verse of scripture has been taken out of context to validate man's religious thoughts about women preachers. And because it has, the Church has missed out on a great deal that women have to offer the Body of Christ. We must stop misinterpreting God's Word because misinterpreting it could mean danger when it comes to a person's life.

First Corinthians chapter 14 and verse 34 for example. Church-going men used this verse to keep the women under control. Misinterpretation of this verse has caused a lot of women to draw back from the call of God for fear of men and this I say is an abomination to God, because God has no respect of persons.

Therefore, if you are a woman and you know that the call of God is on your life to preach and teach His Word, then I encourage you to step out and do what God has called you to do. Of course get the proper training first but do what He has anointed you to do in these last days.

But unto every one of us is given grace according to the measure of the gift of Christ.

Wherefore he saith, when he ascended up on high, he led captivity captive, and gave gifts unto men.

(Now that he ascended, what is it but that he also descended first into the lower parts of the earth?

He that descended is the same also that ascended up far above all heavens, that he might fill all things.)

And he gave some, apostles; and some, prophets; and some, evangelists; and some, pastors and teachers;

For the perfecting of the saints, for the work of the ministry, for the edifying of the body of Christ:
-Ephesians 4:7-12 (KJV)

Ephesians chapter 4 and verse 8 states that God gave [gives] gifts unto men. Now after reading the above verses I know you are saying, "Maurice that passage of scripture states that God gave [gives] gifts unto *men*." Yes, it does and I agree that it says men, but the word "men" in this passage of scripture is defined as "a human being" or "mankind," which includes women. The Beck Translation of this same verse says that God gave [gives] gifts to *people*, my friend, "people" includes women. Therefore, when God passed the gifts [the Anointing of an apostle, prophet, evangelist, pastor and teacher] out to men, He included the women as well. Now if you are a man who has a problem with women preachers, you need to repent and ask God to forgive you for being a respecter of persons—or better yet, for being prejudiced. God Almighty never meant for women to be controlled the way they have been. Let me go a bit further to help you get rid of some of that religious thinking about women in the Church. The Bible tells us that we (the Church) have been called and anointed by God to preach the gospel to the world. It also describes the Church as being the bride of Christ [Jesus].

And he said unto them, Go ye into all the world, and preach the gospel to every creature
-Mark 16:15 (KJV)

And there came unto me one of the seven angels which had the seven vials full of the seven last plagues, and talked with me, saying, Come hither, I will shew thee the bride, the Lamb's wife.

And he carried me away in the spirit to a great and high mountain, and shewed me that great city, the holy Jerusalem, descending out of heaven from God,
-Revelation 21:9-10 (KJV)

With this in mind, I would like to ask a question – In the natural what is the gender [sex] of a bride? Its female [a woman] right? So if the Church is the bride [a women] of Christ, then when God instructed the Church to go into the world and preach the gospel He was commanding His bride to preach. Doesn't that mean He commanded a woman to go preach the Good News? The answer is yes! Therefore, if women were not meant to preach, do you think that God would have instructed His bride to go to preach? I know this analogy seems a bit strange, but the point I am endeavoring to make is this, if God had/has a problem with women preaching, I don't think He would have identified the Church as His bride. Get the picture?

Having said the above let's go back to I Corinthians chapter 14 and verse 34. As I mentioned earlier this particular verse of scripture has been taken out of context in order to control our anointed women. And because of a lack of knowledge, many don't know why Paul had the women keep silent in the Corinthian church. Going back in history you will find that during those days the men sat on the opposite side of the building from their wives during the worship service and many times when something was said by the preacher that the women didn't understand they would blurt out questions to their husbands who were sitting across the room. They did it to get clarification of what was said by the man of God. As a result, Paul had to set order in the church to prevent these distractions from happening.

He instructed the church at Corinth to have their women keep silent in the church, and to wait until they got home to ask their husbands about anything that took place in the church. This was to eliminate the distractions, not because God didn't call women to preach. Keeping women silent in the church is just a religious misinterpretation of the Word that some religious man thought God was saying. Anytime you have religion involved in something it is a guarantee that you will find at least one of three things manifested among the congregation: prejudice, poverty, and racism.

A WORD OF ENCOURAGEMENT

This particular section is for men who are married to women who are called to preach the Word, women who are called to be leaders in the Body of Christ, and not behind the scenes. If this is you I want you to remember one thing that will help you during this wonderful time of transition in the Church, and that is there is neither male nor female when it comes to the call of God on a person's life. What God is looking for in a person is a willing and obedient heart and if that happens to be your wife you should shout Glory to God! I believe that if the wife is called, the husband is called also. However, in this dispensation of time I am noticing that a lot of the women are starting to come to the forefront before their husbands. So what am I saying here? Let me give you an example to help you with this matter. Let's take me for example. I know for a fact that I am called to preach and teach the Word of God and so is my wife. Vinnie and I both are in the ministry but Vinnie started traveling full time with our pastors and crusade team years before I ever had the chance to preach to a congregation.

She was the lead singer on the team and many times she was gone two to three weeks out of a month. As for me I was working with the Federal Government as a Civil Engineer as well as staying home with our three children while Vinnie was on the road ministering the gospel with our church crusade team. Remember I said that God is starting to bring our women to the forefront, and many times it is before their husbands. This could lead to trouble if the man doesn't have the mind of Christ in the matter. Let's take my case for example. For years I thought that since I was the man, God would launch me first into full-time ministry and that my wife would follow and support me in the call that's on my life. Well before I state what I am about to share with you, let me say that that type of thinking created a problem for me when God decided to launch my wife into full-time ministry before me. It was a problem because I was thinking one thing and God was thinking another.

Many times we think "men first and then the women." But that is not always the case when it comes to the call of God on a husband and wife. So I encourage you men to be careful because God just may launch your wife before you, which was the case in my life.

By the way, I was serving in the ministry, but I was not traveling around the world with a crusade team like my wife. Even though we agreed that she could travel with the crusade team, many times I would get frustrated that I wasn't the one leading the way. I would allow stupid stuff to come out of my mouth. Things like "I guess I'm just called to baby sit" and "Why am I only known as Vinnie's husband versus Vinnie being known as my wife?" Stop laughing at me now; I know it was stupid for me to even think that way but I did. A drunkard once told me (when I was ministering to him), "Many times we get stuck on stupid before we decide to do anything right." I was astonished by his statement because I knew in my heart that he was right.

Many times people get stuck on stupid before doing what is right. I hold myself as the prime example. I want to encourage everyone reading these words that you should not allow the enemy to discourage you by having you believe that God has left you out of the big picture. That is not the case at all. To help you get through this change of time or transition, just remember that this is a new day and God is exalting our women to their proper place of ministry.

It is up to us (the husbands) to help and support them (our wives). Even if it means that you have to continue to work on your secular jobs, be home a week or two alone, cook, clean, and take care of the kids while mom is out doing the work of the ministry. Just keep this in your heart and mind: it is okay because God has not forgotten about you.

On the other hand you might not want your wife to do what she is called to do because you feel that cooking, cleaning, and taking care of the kids are a woman's responsibility. Well, I must tell you if you want to prosper and be blessed get rid of that stinking thinking and get with the program. It might be hard at first, but you can do it. I did and glory to God He is blessing me greatly. You might be saying right now, "Maurice, man you don't know what you are talking about." Well my response to your thought is – **YES I DO!** As a matter of fact on April 28, 2000, I was writing the first draft of this book while sitting at a desk in my wife's hotel room in Dallas, Texas. I was visiting her because she had been in a six week crusade at City Church, in Rowlett, Texas. That's right, six weeks. So guess what? I had been Mr. Mom for six weeks and I knew that wasn't going to be the last time I would have to be Mr. Mom. Therefore, I encourage you to *LET YOUR WIFE DO WHAT SHE IS CALLED TO DO!!* Well how can I do that? I am glad you asked, so let me tell you how. Remember, there are three things involved in this situation:

> *1) Know that God hasn't forgotten about you and the call on your life.*
> *2) Know that the call has no gender (sex).*
> *3) Learn to submit to the call on your wife's life.*

These are three keys that will help you get to your next level of ministry.

The most important of the three is number three *LEARN TO SUBMIT TO THE CALL ON YOUR WIFE'S LIFE.* Remember, I am not telling you anything that God hasn't taught me. This revelation has helped me get to the next level in God. So I encourage you to hear what I am saying because it will help you if you receive it as the Word of the Lord.

Now that I have addressed that issue, I want to address submitting to the call. To submit to the call simply means to support your wife in her ministry. Do what it takes to make things easier for her. Make sure she has what she needs for ministry. Be willing to share her with others. Cover her with prayer and faith. Make sure she doesn't put herself in a bad position to be hurt. Do you understand what I am saying here? To put it another way, lay down your life, man of God, so that others might receive life through what God is doing or is going to do through your wife. Learn to esteem others above yourself.

When you submit to what God is doing in your wife's ministry, you are esteeming others above yourself as you share the gift (your wife) with them. Believe me; I know what I am talking about. It gives me so much pleasure to hear how God has touched people's lives through my wife and it is because I've learned not to be selfish, but rather obedient to God.

In the book "Beauty for Ashes" Joyce Meyer explains how her husband, Dave supports her in ministry. If you know anything about Joyce Meyer's Ministry, you know that her husband Dave is in the crowd or behind the scenes somewhere supporting his wife. Man of God, God is not asking you to do something that many of us men are not already doing. So I encourage you once again, yield to the Spirit of God and release your wife to do what she needs to do for God.

If you are a pastor and you want your ministry to grow, take the shackles off your wife, so she can flow freely in the anointing, and forget about what your so-called friends may think of you for letting your wife obey God.

WARNING

Woman of God, if God has launched you into the ministry before your husband (saved or unsaved) you still must obey the Word of God by submitting to your husband's authority. Therefore, if you are planning to succeed in the ministry you must yield to the God-given authority that the Lord has given to your husband.

Wives, submit yourselves unto your own husbands, as unto the Lord.

For the husband is the head of the wife, even as Christ is the head of the church: and he is the saviour of the body
-Ephesians 5:22-23 (KJV)

But Maurice, I thought you said that the husband should submit to the call on his wife's life. Yes, that is exactly what I said, and I am submitted to the call that is on my wife's life, but that doesn't make my wife the head and priest of our home. Being in full-time ministry does not give her the authority to operate as the head and priest of our home and neither does it give you that authority over your husband. Get the picture?

Do not be a JEZEBEL! Stay submitted to your husband's authority. God has placed him there to watch over (not control) you and support you in what He is doing in your life.

"Well my husband has a hard time letting me do what God is telling me to." Well, let me ask you something, "Are you submitting to your husband?" "Are you taking care of your home like you should?" If your answer to these questions is "No" then it is not time for you to go out and minister to anyone, because your first area of ministry is to your family.

That they may teach the young women to be sober, to love their husbands, to love their children,

To be discreet, chaste, keepers at home, good, obedient to their own husbands, that the word of God be not blasphemed
-Titus 2:4-5 (KJV)

I don't care if your husband is saved or unsaved. God still expects you to submit to your husband's authority, provided he's not trying to persuade you to do something that's contrary to the Word of God. This may sound harsh, but it is true; and if you make the proper adjustment in your heart, things will go a lot better for you. In the case where there is a husband who is unsaved, the Bible teaches that your conversation [life style] will sanctify [venerate, purify] your husband.

For the unbelieving husband is sanctified by the wife...
-1 Corinthians 7:14 (KJV)

For perhaps the husband who isn't a Christian may become a Christian with the help of his Christian wife.
-1 Corinthians 7:14 (Tay)

For the heathen husband now belongs to God through his Christian wife
-1 Corinthians 7:14 (NEB)

While it is true that we as men are to submit to our wives as well, according to the Word of God – it is not in the sense that she is the head of the home:

Submitting yourselves one to another in the fear of God.
-Ephesians 5:21 (KJV)

Do not get irritated with me because the emphasis is on you submitting to your husband. I am not trying to prove that God made man the head and priest of the home. However, the emphasis is there to help you fulfill the call on your life. Submitting to your husband's authority will ensure (to God) that you are willing to submit to Him. It is important women of God that you stay submitted to your husband and both of you stay submitted to God, and your pastor who is the shepherd of your souls. You can then watch and see how far God will take you in your ministry.

THE COLOR ISSUE

The next area I want to address is in the area of racism. Earlier I mentioned that the church I attended when I was a kid had no white families (or any other race of people for that matter), as part of the congregation. It is my belief that if a person is a member of an all-black or all-white church, then something is wrong in that body of believers. Now don't get me wrong, there are a few exceptions, especially, if you live in a small town in the middle of the country somewhere. But there are no excuses for people who live in big cities such as Birmingham, Alabama; Pensacola, Florida; New York City; and Los Angeles, California.

You might be saying to yourself, "Well I do not mind if blacks or whites come to my church." My question to you is this – "Are you and your leaders compelling the people to come? People have to feel as though they are a welcome guest before they will come. It is important for the members of the body to go out into the community and compel the people to come. This is only if you want to fully and completely open the door to a multicultural, multifaceted body!

Don't just sit behind the four walls of your building and expect the different races of people to come. You have to make them feel welcome. Open the doors to your church; have some outdoor meetings; knock on the doors of the white people, black people, Chinese, Mexicans, and Jews, etc. Get the picture? You have to be the one to take the first step, and then the people will come.

> *And the Spirit and the bride say, Come. And let him that heareth say, Come. And let him that is athirst come. And whosoever will, let him take the water of life freely*
> **-Revelation 22:17 (KJV)**

> *Come! Say the Spirit and the bride. Come! Let each hearer replay. Come forward, you who are thirsty: accept the water of life, a free gift to all who desire it*
> **-Revelation 22:17 (NEB)**

And the lord said unto the servant, go out into the highways and hedges, and compel them to come in, that my house may be filled
-Luke 14:23 (KJV)

This reminds me of the time when my wife and I were asked by the music minister of the local church we were attending in 1991 and 1992 to take a van load of our youth to Cleveland, Tennessee, to attend a function that was held at a local college there. My wife was a lead singer on the praise team so our minister had made arrangements for her to do a few special songs at this very large Assembly of God Church that was located in city. The church conducted three Sunday morning services and my wife was to sing in each of them.

At the time, this particular church was one of the largest churches my wife and I had ever visited. Now keep in mind that Cleveland, Tennessee is not a small town. What my wife and I observed and experienced that Sunday morning was very shocking. During the time of our visit, the church had been having a revival meeting for about two to three weeks prior to our arrival in the city. On this particular Sunday there were about 1,500 people in each of the services. The first service was held at 8:00 AM and it consisted of the elderly crowd, the retirees; the women who wore the long dresses and had the beehive hairstyles and the men with the sour look on their faces.

The second service began around 10:00 AM and the people who attended were in their early 40's and 50's. This group was more stylish in their dress and a little more lucid than the early morning crowd. The praise and worship was a little more upbeat as well.

The third and final service began at 11:30 AM and ended around 1:00 PM. This service consisted of the people we would call the "Holy Rollers." The praise and worship of the service was a step above that of the second and the majority of the congregation was in their early teens to late 30's.

Each service was packed to the max and the Word was strong. The one thing that really stuck out to my wife and me was that out of the 1500 people there were, only six blacks there and two of them were my wife and me. This large, progressive church congregation was basically a one race church.

My wife and I are very outgoing people, and we can make friends wherever we go because we love people; and we do not consider ourselves to have a racist bone in our bodies. On that Sunday morning, we noticed some very strange things that began to happen in our presence at that large church.

Years ago Vinnie and I made an agreement that we would never sit in the back of a church while a service was being conducted. We always make it our business to get as close to the front as possible so we can hear the Word with no distractions.

On this particular morning we had to go to our hotel after the second service to get our bags for our trip home after the final service. We were running a few minutes late getting back for the third service. When we finally arrived at the church, praise and worship service had already begun. The people were standing to their feet worshipping and praising God. As Vinnie and I walked down the aisle heading for our seats in the second row, something very ungodly began to happen.

People who were praising God—and some were leaders of that church—turned and gave my wife and me a look that said "Why are you here? Who do you think you are? And why are you going to sit up front?" Grant it, we had gotten a few of those looks during the first two services, but they weren't that intense.

Nonetheless, we did not let the looks stop us from going to our seats and praising God. Shortly after their worship was finished, Vinnie was asked to come and sing her special. Once she was finished the guest minister delivered a powerful message that would change people's lives forever. Afterward, the man of God had an alter call for those who wanted to repent for being slack in doing what God had called them to do.

The people stood to their feet but were slow in responding to the call. About five minutes passed before anyone would come up, but after a few more words from the man of God, a hand full of people began to make their way to the altar. What I am about to share with you could come as a shock, but it happened.

As I stood near my seat during the altar call with my eyes closed all the while thanking God for what He was doing. Suddenly I felt something tugging at my left arm trying to get me to raise it up. I opened my eyes to see what was going on. As I did, I noticed that it was a young man who was about nineteen or twenty years of age. It was obvious he was one of the local college students who had made his way up front in response to the altar call. As the young man stood by me, he took my left arm and put it around his shoulder as if he was my son. As I allowed him to, he laid his head on me and began to weep because of the presence of the Lord. The young man's action and my response to his action caused a ripple effect in the building. What the people saw that day was the love of God crossing racial barriers. This episode shocked the entire congregation, because as I put my arms around this guy with no hesitation, the people—even one or two of the leaders—began to *oooo* and *aaah* at what they were seeing. Initially I didn't know why the people responded the way they did, but then it hit me that I was black and the young man was white.

The congregation was not accustomed to seeing anything like that and I never felt so out of place in my life. However, I continued to stand there with my arm around him. As I did my wife and I got some even stranger looks, but we were at peace because we knew that God was using us to prove a point and to break down some walls among that body of saints. God was trying to get those people out of their racist mode in order to bless them.

There we stood among 1500 people that claimed to love God; yet some had a problem with me - a black man, ministering to a young white male the way the Lord instructed me to. These kinds of occurrences are not isolated. They still go on in churches today! Saints are still separating themselves because of color.

Years later, my wife and I decided to visit a church that her brother and sister attend in Birmingham, Alabama. It is a large church that sat about 500–700 people in any one service. Due to the number of members it was necessary to conduct two Sunday morning services. The service we attended was filled; every seat was taken. My wife and I both agreed that the praise and worship was great and the teaching was great. But there was one thing wrong. Out of 500–700 people there was only one white lady present. As large as Birmingham is, there should have been more than just that one white lady in the congregation, but there was not. Why? Because, the members of that church were not compelling other nationalities to come and be a part their church body.

For years the church has been the most segregated place there is and that is sad. But a transition has taken place in the realm of the spirit and multicultural churches are springing up around the world. People who are in pursuit of the things of God have stepped beyond the racial barriers that once stood in their way. Glory to God the walls of racism are coming down!

In Acts chapters 10 through 11 the Word plainly tells us that we should not call that which is cleansed by God unclean. We the saints of God have been cleansed by the Blood of the Lamb and the Word of God. So what is the point? If you are a black American and have a problem with someone of another race being in the same congregation as you, then you have just called that race of people unclean in your own mind. Vice/versa. If you are a white American and have a problem with being in the same congregation with someone of another race.

> *But if we walk in the light, as he is in the light, we have fellowship one with another, and the blood of Jesus Christ his Son cleanseth us from all sin*
>
> *-I John 1:7 (KJV)*

We as children of God should not have a problem fellowshipping and worshipping with our brothers and sisters in the Lord who are of a different race. We should always walk in love toward them and forget about the problems our forefathers had with one another. Why? Because the love of God doesn't see color and it has no problem crossing racial barriers. First John chapter 4 and verse 20 states that a person that claims he loves God yet hates his brother is a liar. According to the Strong's Concordance the word "liar" is the word "psyoostace" in the Greek, which is defined as "one who is a falsifier." The word "psyoostace" is derived from the Greek word "psyoodomanee" which means "to attempt to deceive by falsehood."

Therefore, if a person is prejudiced toward his/her black or white sister or brother in the Lord, but claims that he/she loves God he/she is deceiving himself/herself through falsehood. In other words, he/she is deceiving himself/herself through lack of accuracy or truth of the Word of God.

> *If a man say I love God, and hateth his brother, he is a liar: for he that loveth not his brother whom he hath seen, how can he love God whom he hath not seen?*
>
> *-I John 4:20 (KJV)*

> *For if a man think himself to be something, when he is nothing, he deceiveth himself*
>
> *-Galatians 6:3 (KJV)*

THE RISING OF THE GIANT

Once I heard a pastor share a vision she had years ago. In the vision she saw a giant lying on his back with his head toward the South Pole and his feet toward the North Pole. The giant was bound with ropes and covered with debris. Even though he was bound, the giant would shake himself in an attempt to free himself from the bondage that kept him bound. As the vision was told the giant made several attempts to free himself in his own power; but he was unsuccessful because he lacked the necessary strength and power he needed to do so.

Several minutes later in the vision, the giant began to shake himself more violently until all the ropes and debris fell from his body. Freeing himself, the giant stood to his feet. Standing on top of the globe, the giant was very large and tall in statue and appeared to have great strength and power. For several minutes the giant stood in all of his power and glory. Suddenly something amazing took place. The giant began to dissolve into a multitude of people who went into every part of the world. They began to run and scatter to the north, south, east, and west sectors of the globe. Our church congregation began to rejoice and shout about what was being revealed to us. The atmosphere of the meeting was charged with the presence and power of God as the vision was shared with the church body. After the dissolving of the giant, the Lord began to explain that the giant represented the Church and that the debris and ropes that bound him represented the cares of life, false doctrine, religion, and the doubt and unbelief that robbed the church of her strength and power. The Lord went on to explain the cause of the giant shaking violently to free himself: he was beginning to realize who he was and what he had in Christ Jesus. As the giant began to receive revelation knowledge about himself the power of the Word began to fill his heart to the point where he was able to free himself from the things that had bound him for so many years.

Now the multitude that appeared after the dissolving of the giant represents the people who make up the Body of Christ. These are the people who will rise up and take dominion in the earth – the ones who will go into the world preaching, teaching, casting out devils, and laying hands on the sick. They represent the remnant of people who are going to do the greater works than Christ in these last days.

For we are members of his body, of his flesh, and of his bones
-Ephesians 5:30 (KJV)

So we, numerous as we are, are one body in Christ (the Messiah) and individually we are parts one of another [mutually dependent on one another]
-Romans 12:5 (Amp)

And he said unto them, Go ye into all the world, and preach the gospel to every creature.

He that believeth and is baptized shall be saved; but he that believeth not shall be damned.

And these signs shall follow them that believe; In my name shall they cast out devils; they shall speak with new tongues;

They shall take up serpents; and if they drink any deadly thing, it shall not hurt them; they shall lay hands on the sick, and they shall recover
-Mark 16:15-18 (KJV)

Verily, verily, I say unto you, He that believeth on me, the works that I do shall he do also; and greater works than these shall he do; because I go unto my Father
-John 14:12 (KJV)

They were the people who represent you and me. The very elect of God, the mighty men and women of valour, the giant killers and city takers, people who know who they are in Christ, the called-out ones and people of faith who have been trained and equipped for the work of the ministry.

And he gave some, apostles; and some, prophets; and some, evangelists; and some, pastors and teachers;

For the perfecting of the saints, for the work of the ministry, for the edifying of the body of Christ:
-Ephesians 4:11-12 (KJV)

The Bible tells us that we are to *let every word be established out of the mouth of two or three witnesses* (Matthew 18:16). On June 6, 2000 while ministering to our congregation Pastor Mark Brazee told us about a man of God by the name of Tommy Hicks. Tommy Hicks was a man who flowed in the miracles, signs, and wonders of God. During his ministry God showed him a dream similar to the one I explained earlier.

According to Pastor Brazee, Tommy Hicks dreamed of this giant three nights in a row because God was showing him that there would be a day coming when the giant (the Church) would arise and be what God has called us to be. I would say that the first vision I spoke to you about was confirmation to what God had already revealed to his man of God many years before. We are in transition. Our phase of transitioning is from being a weak and powerless Church to developing into and becoming a bold and powerful Church.

THE BLIND LEADING THE BLIND

Not that which goeth into the mouth defileth a man; but that which cometh out of the mouth, this defileth a man. Then came his disciples, and said unto him, Knowest thou that the Pharisees were offended, after they heard this saying? But he answered and said, Every plant, which my heavenly Father hath not planted, shall be rooted up. Let them alone: they be blind leaders of the blind. And if the blind lead the blind, both shall fall into the ditch
-Matthew 7-14 (KJV)

Then came to Jesus scribes and Pharisees, which were of Jerusalem, saying,
Why do thy disciples transgress the tradition of the elders, for they wash not their hands when they eat bread.

But he answered and said unto them. Why do ye also transgress the commandment of God by your tradition?

Ye hypocrites, well did Esaias prophesy of you, saying,

This people draweth nigh unto me with their mouth, and honoureth me with their lips; but their heart is far from me.

> *But in vain they do worship me, teaching for doctrines the*
> *commandments of men.*
>
> *And he called the multitude, and said unto them, hear and understand:*
> **-Matthew 15:1-3 and 7-10 (KJV)**

Earlier in this chapter I mentioned that for years the Church has been living in darkness, doubt, and unbelief. It is sad to say but one reason for this is that the pulpits around the globe, and especially in the good ole USA, have been filled with mama- and daddy-called preachers. These men are self-made or man-made preachers. They are preachers that know nothing about the Word of God or how He operates by His Spirit.

These so-called preachers are blind guides who have nothing to offer to the men and women of the world; and needless to say, even less to the Church. They are filled with hot air and capable of feeding people only contaminated food. In the Bible, these men were known as the scribes and Pharisees, or better yet, hypocrites.

The Strong's Concordance defines a "hypocrite" as "someone who is acting under an assumed character" or "a stage player." In other words, someone who is a phony or an impostor, or a wolf in sheep's clothing who preaches only for selfish gain.

> *Beware of false prophets, which come to you in sheep's clothing, but*
> *inwardly they are ravening wolves*
> **-Matthew 7:15 (KJV)**
>
> *For false Christs and false prophets shall rise, and shall shew signs*
> *and wonders, to seduce, if it were possible, even the elect*
> **-Mark 13:22 (KJV)**

They have caused great damage to the Body of Christ because they only preach and teach for doctrine the commandments of men, not the commandments of God. These commandments are nothing more than mom and pop sermons that they have heard someone else preach – messages that were passed down through generations of dead beats. This type of preaching has kept millions from coming to know the Lord Jesus Christ and I would endeavor to say that many have died and gone to hell because of these vipers and stage player leaders.

Over the years, the devil has used these so-called leaders to destroy the lives of people around the world through their religious and poison-filled teaching. Alas, there is good news! The days of mom and pop sermons are over. This is a new day and God is removing these snakes from the midst of His people. Their works are starting to come down. Why? Because the Bible tells us that if a man's work is of God, it will stand through the fire of God; and if it is not of God, then that man will suffer loss or be destroyed. In other words, a man-made kingdom will fall to the ground.

These ungodly leaders are being replaced by men and women of God who have been mentored and trained for the work of the ministry – men who are called of God and not called of mom and dad.

For we are fellow workman (joint promoters, laborers together) with and for God; you are God's garden and vineyard and field under cultivation, [you are] God's building.

According to the grace (the special Endowment for my task) God bestowed on me, like a Skillful architect and master builder I laid [the] foundation, and now another [man] is building upon it But let each [man] be careful how he builds upon it,

For no other foundation can anyone lay than that which is [already] laid, which is Jesus Christ (the Messiah, the Anointed One).

But if anyone builds upon the Foundation, whether it be with gold, silver, precious stones, wood, hay, straw,

The work of each [one] will become [plainly, openly] known (shown for what it is); for the day [of Christ] will disclose and declare it, because it will be revealed with fire, and the fire will test and critically appraise the character and worth of the work each person has done.

If the work which any person has built on this Foundation [any product of his efforts whatever] survives [this test], he will get his rewarded.

But if any person's work is burned up [under the test], he will suffer the loss [of it all, losing his reward], though he himself will be saved, but only as [one who has passed] through the fire.

Do you not discern and understand that you [the whole church at Corinth] are God's temple (His sanctuary), and that God's Spirit has His permanent dwelling in you [to be home in you, collectively as a church and also individually]?

If anyone does hurt to God's temple or corrupts it [with false doctrines] or destroys it, God will do hurt to him and bring him the corruption of death and destroy him. For the temple of God is holy (sacred to Him) and that [temple] you [the believing church and its individual believers] are.

-I Corinthians 3:9-17 (Amp)

A new generation of leaders is being sent out by their spiritual fathers. Notice I said **"sent"** and not **"went."** You see, many pulpits today are infested and occupied by men who went out and were not sent out. They went out on their own for selfish reasons and selfish gain. In the process of building their own little kingdom, they wounded and scared many souls with their forked tongues. But thank God for the men and women who are taking the Word of God at face value and changing the lives of people around the world.

People like Dr. Creflo and Taffi Dollar, and Dr. Kenneth and Gloria Copeland, just to name a few – are men and women of faith who have all proven the Word of God in their own lives and ministries. They are examples of ministers who were sent by God to deliver his message for the ultimate purpose of healing our land and encouraging the saints.

As they ministered to the Lord, and fasted, the Holy Ghost said, separate me Barnabas and Saul for the work whereunto I have called them.

And when they had fasted and prayed, and laid their hands on them, they sent them away.

So they, being sent forth by the Holy Ghost, departed unto Seleucia; and from thence they sailed to Cyprus.

-Acts 13:2-4 (KJV)

If you are a pastor that would like to have a move of God, I encourage you to have the above ministries come to your church. I have witnessed the power of God on these ministries and once you come in contact with the anointing on them, you will never be the same.

If you are not sure about them because of something you heard, be assured that you can count that report as a lie, and get them in your church because they are truly men and women of revival! It is because of them that people around the world are getting understanding and revelation of God's Word. God is by His Spirit expelling darkness by the light of His Word and those who have compromised the Word for one reason or another and call themselves ministers of the Gospel are starting to fall like dead trees.

Their work is drying up like the desert because there is no life in what they are preaching. Most of these false preachers, or wolves in shepherd's clothing, have used manipulation for years to keep people bound by religion. They teach that healing is not for today and that God keeps people broke to humble them. They are preachers who are not concerned about what they can do for the people, but rather what the people can do for them.

They are men and women who have a form of godliness but deny the power thereof (2 Timothy 3:5). God is setting his people free from these lukewarm modern day scribes and Pharisees.

The Strong's Concordance defines the word "lukewarm" as "the condition of the soul wretchedly fluctuating between torpor and fervors of love." In other words, lukewarmness is the condition of the mind, will, and emotions of a person who is deeply distressed or unhappy, miserable, and unfortunate; one who is continually changing or varying in an irregular way concerning the things of God. They are in a state of being dormant or inactive, and they have temporarily lost all or part of the power of sensation to the intense heat of God.

However, the Church is in transition and God is extracting the lukewarm from the pulpits and from the public eye. He is spewing [vomiting] them out of His mouth and replacing them with men and women who will not compromise the power of the Word for selfish gain and selfish motives.

I know thy works that thou art neither cold nor hot: I would thou wert cold or hot.

So then because thou art lukewarm, and neither cold nor hot, I will spew thee out of my mouth.

Because thou sayest, I am rich, and increased with goods, and have need of nothing; and knowest not that thou art wretched, and miserable, and poor, and blind, and naked:

-Revelation 3:15-17 (KJV)

THE MULTITUDES ARE COMING

Over the years the people of the world have run away from the Church. They have done so because of doom and gloom religious preaching, the type of preaching that has kept the Church in sickness, lack, and bondage. However, change has come to the Body of Christ.

The Spirit of God is reviving the Church and confirming His Word with miracles, signs, and wonders. Therefore, the world is starting to see an alive, rich, healthy, and prosperous Church because of the glory of God that has come upon her.

For years the world only saw a bunch of defeated people who where clothed in false humility and poverty. People who were trained to believe that God made them sick to teach them something and made them broke to humble them. But a transition is taking place and the glory of this latter house is starting to become greater than that of the former. The light of God is starting to shine on and through the Church body and the world is starting to see what the Bible calls "the resurrected and glorious Church."

The 60th chapter of the book of Isaiah states that darkness shall cover the earth and gross darkness will cover the people. But the Lord will arise upon His people and His glory shall be seen upon them.

The glory of this latter house shall be greater than of the former, saith the LORD of hosts: and in this place will I give peace, saith the LORD of hosts

-Haggai 2:9 (KJV)

Ye are the light of the world. A city that is set on an hill cannot be hid.

Neither do men light a candle, and put it under a bushel, but on a candlestick; and it giveth light unto all that are in the house.

Let your light so shine before men, that they may see your good works, and glorify your Father which is in heaven
-Matthew 5:14-16 (KJV)

Arise, shine; for thy light is come, and the glory of the LORD is risen upon thee.

For, behold, the darkness shall cover the earth, and gross darkness the people: but the LORD shall arise upon thee, and his glory shall be seen upon thee.

And the Gentiles shall come to thy light, and kings to the brightness of thy rising.

Lift up thine eyes round about, and see: all they gather themselves together, they come to thee: thy sons shall come from far, and thy daughters shall be nursed at thy side.

Then thou shalt see, and flow together, and thine heart shall fear, and be enlarged; because the abundance of the sea shall be converted unto thee, the forces of the Gentiles shall come unto thee.
-Isaiah 60:1-5 (KJV)

The amplified version of Isaiah 60:1-5 states that nations will be drawn to the Church because she has arisen from the depressed state that once kept her bound. In other words, the Lord is shining upon His body so strongly that nations are starting to come with their wealth. (This transition of wealth will be discussed in a later chapter). So I encourage you to let your light shine to its fullest capacity so that the world will see and know that you are God's.

CHAPTER V

TRANSFERENCE OF WEALTH

I f you have a problem with men and women of God having money or you believe that money is evil, then I advise you not to read any further, because this chapter is not for you. On the other hand, if you believe that the wealth of the wicked has been stored up for the just (Proverbs 13:22), then continue to read this chapter, because God has something special for you.

Earlier I mentioned that there is a transition that has begun to take place in the Body of Christ, mainly because the Church has received more revelation knowledge about herself in the areas of who she is and what she has in Christ.

In this chapter I am going to deal with something that is very important to the Body of Christ and that is money. That's right – *MONEY!* Why money? Because it is going to take lots of it to get the Gospel of Christ to the world.

Each year it takes ministries millions of dollars to televise their programs and to fly to different cities and countries to conduct massive crusades where millions of souls are being saved. The church needs to know the purpose of wealth and also get a revelation of the transference that has already begun to take place.

Before you can reap from what I am about to share with you, you must first empty yourself of everything negative you have learned concerning money. Things like: money is the root of all evil, we should not accept drug money in the church offering, or money is dirty. Having these thoughts have caused many of God's people to suffer unnecessarily; not to mention the preachers who have had to work secular jobs to support their families.

Money is not dirty or evil, and neither can it do more than what we use it for. It is the love (lust) of money that is the root of all evil and not the money itself. Money is only a tool that God has put here for us to use as a means of trade.

> *For the love of money is the root of all evil: which while some coveted after, they have erred from the faith, and pierced themselves through with many sorrows.*
>
> *-I Timothy 6:10 (KJV)*

If the possessor of the money has an evil heart, then nine times out of ten, the money will be used for evil purposes. On the other hand, if the possessor of the money is a born again believer who has a pure and clean heart, then that same money will be used for godly purposes.

I like the statement Dennis Burke made concerning wealth in his June 2000 "Word to the Wise" monthly magazine. He said, "Money only amplifies the inner qualities someone already possesses. Money itself is not the root of evil but the wrong attachment or affection for what wealth can do will open a person to Satan's strategies."

Money is not dirty or evil. So remember, it is the love (lust) of money that is the root of all evil. There are people today who will steal, kill, and destroy others just to get a dollar or two. The pimps, the pornographers, the abortionists, and the drug dealers are just a few examples of the people who lust after money.

According to the Strong's Concordance "lust (for money)" is defined as "to have too great a desire (to have wealth); greed (for riches); or to have a strong desire (for wealth)." Once again there is nothing wrong with having money, but as Christians we should not make money our first priority. We should not lust after money like the world does. In First Timothy chapter 6 and verses 9–10, Paul advises Timothy about Christians who covet or seek after wealth. He states that these people have erred from the faith and pierced themselves through with many sorrows.

But they that will be rich fall into temptation and a snare, and into many foolish and hurtful lusts, which drown men in destruction and perdition.

For the love of money is the root of all evil: which while some coveted after, they have erred from the faith, and pierced themselves through with many sorrows.

-I Timothy 6:9-10 (KJV)

In other words, that man or woman of God has been lead astray from the truth by seeking after money, and because they have, their souls are tortured with consuming pain and sorrow. It is sad to say but I notice Christians nearly every day seeking after riches. They are consumed with the thought of money to the point that they rob God just to keep a dollar or two in their pockets. This should not be; we are instructed to seek the kingdom of God first and His righteousness and everything else will be added to us.

But seek ye first the kingdom of God, and his righteousness; and all these things shall be added unto you.

-Matthew 6:33 (KJV)

Please realize that the intent of this chapter is not to get you so worked up about money that you can't think about anything else. The intent is to help you understand that even though God wants you rich, He does not want the wealth He has in store for you to become your god. We should at all times remember that money is not the source of joy. There are many people today who believe that if they had millions of dollars everything would be okay and all of their problems would just fade away.

People with this mentality are living in fantasy land. If money could take away people's problems, then why do most of our entertainers have the problems they do? Howard Hughes was one of the richest men in the world, yet he lived alone and died a miserable man. Money is not the answer, Jesus is!

Only God can give us the joy we need, because He is joy. We must be very careful with the wealth that is entering our hands. Before the children of God left Egypt, God had them borrow from the Egyptians. This was a type and shadow of the wealth being transferred to God's people today.

And I will give this people favour in the sight of the Egyptians: and it shall come to pass, that, when ye go, ye shall not go empty:

But every woman shall borrow of her neighbour, and of her that sojourneth in her house, jewels of silver, and jewels of gold, and raiment: and ye shall put them upon your sons, and upon your daughters; and ye shall spoil the Egyptians.
-Exodus 3:21-22 (KJV)

Now I am not encouraging you to go and charge up credit cards and make loans that you have no intention of paying back. *NO!* If you borrow money and charge up your credit cards *PAY YOUR BILLS!* However, I am using this illustration to show you that God had the wealth of the wicked transferred to His people. Unfortunately they made a god out of it. We are told in First Timothy chapter 6 and verse 17 not to trust in uncertain riches because you cannot serve two masters unless you put one before the other. So be careful and never make the mistake of making money a god by putting it before our Lord and Savior Jesus Christ.

And all the people brake off the golden earrings which were in their ears, and brought them unto Aaron.

And he received them at their hand, and fashioned it with a graving tool, after he had made it a molten calf: and they said, These be thy gods, O Israel, which brought thee up out of the land of Egypt.
-Exodus 32:3-4 (KJV)

Thou shalt have no other gods before me.

Thou shalt not make unto thee any graven image, or any likeness of anything that is in heaven above, or that is in the earth beneath, or that is in the water under the earth:
-Exodus 20:3-4 (KJV)

No man can serve two masters: for either he will hate the one, and love the other; or else he will hold to the one, and despise the other. Ye cannot serve God and mammon.

-Matthew 6:24 (KJV)

Wealth Defined

...But thou shalt remember the LORD thy God: for it is he that giveth thee power to get wealth, that he may establish his covenant which he sware unto thy fathers, as it is this day.

-Deuteronomy 8:18 (KJV)

So what exactly is wealth? Well I like the way I heard someone put it years ago. He said, "Wealth is whatever is necessary to establish the covenant." You see, in this day and time when people hear the word "wealth" they automatically think of money only, but money is just a small portion of what God considers wealth. Note, that in the days of old, wealth did not mean money only; wealth also meant gold, silver, livestock, and other possessions.

For example, the Bible tells us that Abraham was rich in possessions; he owned 300 head of sheep as well as other livestock. According to Webster's Dictionary "wealth" is defined as "all property, possessions, and monetary value." The cars we drive and even the shoes we own would be considered wealth in some parts of the world. Let me give you an example of what I mean.

In 1998 my wife and I had the opportunity to accompany our pastors to the Philippines to conduct a massive crusade. This was the first time that my wife and I ever visited a third world country. Upon our arrival we immediately realized how blessed we were as Americans.

What we saw in that country was shocking. The environment of the city was so poverty-stricken that the whole country—in my book—should have been vacated and condemned. We saw activities that we thought only existed on television. There were people living in shacks along contaminated ditches, the air had a stench from the open sewer, and we observed little kids with no clothes playing with sickly looking pets.

The economy of that country was really bad. At that time, the American dollar was worth forty to forty-five pesos. Now Vinnie and I have seen some ghettos here in America but nothing compared to what we saw in Manila. The mindset of the people was unbelievable. For example, when the cab driver dropped us off at our hotel there in Manila, my pastor offered him 100 pesos for a tip. Immediately a look of fear came over the driver's face as if someone were robbing him instead of trying to bless him.

The cab driver was afraid to receive the money from a person who was trying to bless. Instead of receiving the blessing, he refused it because he felt it was too much for him to accept as a tip. Realize what I am saying here. The 100 pesos was less than two dollars in American currency; yet it was too much for that nice gentleman to accept as a tip for his services. Later I learned that 100 pesos was more than the cab driver made in a month.

At the time of our visit to the Philippines, I was making a little over $1000 per week as a civil engineer with the United States Department of Defense. Knowing that cab drivers made less than two dollars per month in Manila, I began to wonder just how much an engineer with my experience made in that country.

Doing a little research on my own, I later found out that an engineer with my experience made anywhere between 400 and 600 pesos per month. That is ten to fifteen dollars per month in our country. That means that a person who makes $50,000 per year in American currency would be the equivalent of a millionaire in the Philippines, because $50,000 is worth 2,000,000 pesos in Manila currency. Amazing, isn't it?

It was sad but it helped my wife and I realize that we are really blessed to have what we have in the United States. We also realized that over the years we had done nothing but complain about what we didn't have instead of thanking God for what He had already blessed us with. I told my wife and pastors that even if a person is living on food stamps and getting welfare here in the states, they need to keep their mouth closed at all times because they are living better than most people in the world, particularly the people of Manila.

We should always thank God for what we have, especially if we are Christians. Sometimes I believe that we act worse than the average sinner when it comes to being ungrateful. Many times our prayers consist of telling God about what we don't have and what He should give us to make our lives happier. Instead, I encourage you to do this the next time you want to complain to God about what you don't have: think about the people in the Philippines. Hopefully that will help you realize how blessed you really are and motivate you to thank God for what He has already done in your life.

Wealth does not consist of having money only. Real wealth is having the power of God operating and functioning in your life. It is that power that gives you the ability to get the wealth.

But thou shalt remember the LORD thy God: for it is he that giveth thee power to get wealth, that he may establish his covenant which he sware unto thy fathers, as it is this day.
-Deuteronomy 8:18 (KJV)

THE WEALTH OF THE WICKED

A good man leaveth an inheritance to his children's children: and the wealth of the sinner is laid up for the just.
-Proverbs 13:22 (KJV)

In the above verse of scripture we learn that the wealth (the goods, riches, or substance of the sinner) has been laid up for the just. The Septuagint Translation of the above verse puts it this way: "…the wealth of the wicked is treasured up for the righteous." This tells you and me that the riches they (the sinner) have in their possession by scheming, killing, and vanity have been gathered up for God's people for these last days. Also the monies that you and I have worked for but were under paid will be given back to us. Shocking isn't it? But it is true. The Bible tells us that the wages that have been kept back by fraud by our employers have cried out to the Lord to be restored to us.

Go to now, ye rich men, weep and howl for your miseries that shall come upon you.

Your riches are corrupted, and your garments are motheaten.

Your gold and silver is cankered; and the rust of them shall be a witness against you, and shall eat your flesh as it were fire. Ye have heaped treasure together for the last days.

Behold, the hire of the labourers who have reaped down your fields, which is of you kept back by fraud, crieth: and the cries of them which have reaped are entered into the ears of the Lord of sabaoth.
-James 5:1-4 (KJV)

According to the Strong's Concordance, the word "hire" in the above passage of scripture is the word "misthos" in the Greek, which means "rewards, wages, or dues paid for work." I will give you an example of this scripture. Years ago I received an e-mail from one of my previous supervisors. The e-mail stated that a class action lawsuit had been filed by the union that represents The Department of Defense (DOD) Engineers and Scientists. The union was suing the government for back pay due to all Engineers and Scientists who started working with the DOD between the years 1982 and 1988. It was during this time that the government was trying to give their engineers a salary that was equivalent to private sector engineer, but they had failed in their efforts. They had to go back and pay those of us who started work with them during those years the difference between what we were making and what we were supposed to make. The key about this matter is that my supervisor knew about the lawsuit the day it was filed, but I knew nothing about it. But God knew. So after my pastor taught on James chapter 5 and verses 1–4, I began to confess it over my life and when I did, it wasn't long before I received the e-mail informing me of the back pay I would be receiving a few months later.

BIBLICAL ACCOUNTS OF THE TRANSFERENCE OF WEALTH

The Lord causes, and is now causing the sinner to heap up that which belongs to us. A good example of this is found in the book of Exodus when God told Moses to have the Israelites borrow jewels and gold from the Egyptians before their deliverance. The Egyptians had become very wealthy during the time they held Israel captive. It was because of the Israelites' slave labor that the Egyptians became wealthy. That wealth was taken from God's people by fraud, but God made sure that His people got what belonged to them before they were freed from Egypt.

And the LORD said unto Moses, Yet will I bring one plague more upon Pharaoh, and upon Egypt; afterwards he will let you go hence: when he shall let you go, he shall surely thrust you out hence altogether.

Speak now in the ears of the people, and let every man borrow of his neighbour, and every woman of her neighbour, jewels of silver, and jewels of gold.

And the LORD gave the people favour in the sight of the Egyptians. Moreover the man Moses was very great in the land of Egypt, in the sight of Pharaoh's servants, and in the sight of the people.
-Exodus 11:1-3 (KJV)

In order to help your faith, I have included the following scriptures to illustrate how God is going to use the wicked to transfer the wealth into the hands of His people for this end time harvest. I encourage you to meditate on them until they become a part of your spirit so that you can be prepared for the wealth that is about to come your way.

For thus saith the LORD of hosts; Yet once, it is a little while, and I will shake the heavens, and the earth, and the sea, and the dry land;

And I will shake all nations, and the desire of all nations shall come: and I will fill this house with glory, saith the LORD of hosts.

The silver is mine, and the gold is mine, saith the LORD of hosts.

The glory of this latter house shall be greater than of the former, saith the LORD of hosts: and in this place will I give peace, saith the LORD of hosts.
-Haggai 2:6-9 (KJV)

Arise, shine; for thy light is come, and the glory of the LORD is risen upon thee.

For, behold, the darkness shall cover the earth, and gross darkness the people: but the LORD shall arise upon thee, and his glory shall be seen upon thee.

And the Gentiles shall come to thy light, and kings to the brightness of thy rising.

Lift up thine eyes round about, and see: all they gather themselves together, they come to thee: thy sons shall come from far, and thy daughters shall be nursed at thy side.

Then thou shalt see, and flow together, and thine heart shall fear, and be enlarged; because the abundance of the sea shall be converted unto thee, the forces of the Gentiles shall come unto thee.

The multitude of camels shall cover thee, the dromedaries of Midian and Ephah; all they from Sheba shall come: they shall bring gold and incense; and they shall shew forth the praises of the LORD.

All the flocks of Kedar shall be gathered together unto thee, the rams of Nebaioth shall minister unto thee: they shall come up with acceptance on mine altar, and I will glorify the house of my glory.

-Isaiah 60:1-7 (KJV)

Be glad then, ye children of Zion, and rejoice in the LORD your God: for he hath given you the former rain moderately, and he will cause to come down for you the rain, the former rain, and the latter rain in the first month.

And the floors shall be full of wheat, and the fats shall overflow with wine and oil.

And I will restore to you the years that the locust hath eaten, the cankerworm, and the caterpiller, and the palmerworm, my great army which I sent among you.

And ye shall eat in plenty, and be satisfied, and praise the name of the LORD your God, that hath dealt wondrously with you: and my people shall never be ashamed.

And ye shall know that I am in the midst of Israel, and that I am the LORD your God, and none else: and my people shall never be ashamed.

-Joel 2:23-27 (KJV)

Again the word of the LORD came unto me, saying...

I have caused thee to multiply as the bud of the field, and thou hast increased and waxen great, and thou art come to excellent ornaments: thy breasts are fashioned, and thine hair is grown, whereas thou wast naked and bare.

Now when I passed by thee, and looked upon thee, behold, thy time was the time of love; and I spread my skirt over thee, and covered thy nakedness: yea, I sware unto thee, and entered into a covenant with thee, saith the Lord GOD, and thou becamest mine.

Then washed I thee with water; yea, I throughly washed away thy blood from thee, and I anointed thee with oil.

I clothed thee also with broidered work, and shod thee with badgers' skin, and I girded thee about with fine linen, and I covered thee with silk.

I decked thee also with ornaments, and I put bracelets upon thy hands, and a chain on thy neck.

And I put a jewel on thy forehead, and earrings in thine ears, and a beautiful crown upon thine head.

> *Thus wast thou decked with gold and silver; and thy raiment was of fine linen, and silk, and broidered work; thou didst eat fine fl our, and honey, and oil: and thou wast exceeding beautiful, and thou didst prosper into a kingdom.*
>
> *And thy renown went forth among the heathen for thy beauty: for it was perfect through my comeliness, which I had put upon thee, saith the Lord GOD.*
>
> *-Ezekiel 16:1 and 7-14 (KJV)*

POSITIONING YOURSELF FOR THE TRANSFERENCE OF WEALTH

In today's society wealth is a very sensitive issue, especially in the church. As I mentioned earlier, many will do anything to get it—sinner and saint alike. However, if you are sincere about the things of God, God will cause the wealth that many have strived for to flow your way if you are in a position to receive it.

You and I must position ourselves to receive the wealth that God has in store for us. Many believers think that they can do anything and live any way and still receive the blessings of God. But that is not true. God will only bless those of us who are obedient to His Word. He is not going to bless a thief with money. Don't forget that we are talking about money here and I want you to understand that God is only going to put the wealth of the wicked into the hands of those who understand, or have a revelation of, what how this wealth is to be utilized.

It is very important for you to understand what I am saying here. So please allow me to help you.

THINGS TO REMEMBER

Below I have listed a few things that you and I should remember in order to position ourselves to receive the blessings of the Lord in our lives. Follow carefully as I give you a few pointers to remember about wealth.

1. Remember to tithe. It is not a suggestion; it is a commandment by God.

Bring ye all the tithes into the storehouse, that there may be meat in mine house, and prove me now herewith, saith the LORD of hosts, if I will not open you the windows of heaven, and pour you out a blessing, that there shall not be room enough to receive it.

-Malachi 3:10 (KJV)

2. Remember you must sow in order to reap.

Give, and it shall be given unto you; good measure, pressed down, and shaken together, and running over, shall men give into your bosom. For with the same measure that ye mete withal it shall be measured to you again.

-Luke 6:38 (KJV)

3. Remember that giving of our substance is an act of praise and worship.

Honour the LORD with thy substance, and with the first fruits of all thine increase:

-Proverbs 3:9 (KJV)

4. Remember that God is the one who multiplies your seed sown.

Now he that ministereth seed to the sower both minister bread for your food, and multiply your seed sown, and increase the fruits of your righteousness;

-2 Corinthians 9:10 (KJV)

5. Remember that the purpose of this wealth is to establish God's covenant with mankind.

But thou shalt remember the LORD thy God: for it is he that giveth thee power to get wealth, that he may establish his covenant which he sware unto thy fathers, as it is this day.

-Deuteronomy 8:18 (KJV)

6. Remember that all the wealth in the world is the Lord's.

For the earth is the Lord's, and the fullness thereof
-1 Corinthians 10:26 (KJV)

The silver is mine, and the gold is mine, saith the LORD of hosts.
-Haggai 2:8 (KJV)

7. Remember that money is not evil, the lust of it is evil.

For the love of money is the root of all evil: which while some coveted after, they have erred from the faith, and pierced themselves through with many sorrows.
-1 Timothy 6:10 (KJV)

8. Remember that the wealth you are about to receive is part of your inheritance as a child of God.

So then they which be of faith are blessed with faithful Abraham...

For ye are all the children of God by faith in Christ Jesus...

And if ye be Christ's, then are ye Abraham's seed, and heirs according to the promise
-Galatians 3:9, 26 and 29 (KJV)

9. Remember never to seek riches but to always seek the kingdom of God.

Therefore take no thought, saying, What shall we eat? or, What shall we drink? or, Wherewithal shall we be clothed?

(For after all these things do the Gentiles seek:) for your heavenly Father knoweth that ye have need of all these things.

But seek ye first the kingdom of God, and his righteousness; and all these things shall be added unto you. Take therefore no thought for the morrow: for the morrow shall take thought for the things of itself.

-Matthew 6:31-33 (KJV)

10. Remember never to put your trust in riches.

He that trusteth in his riches shall fall: but the righteous shall flourish as a branch.

-Proverbs 11:28 (KJV)

The above items are just a few things that I have learned over the years as a child of God. Meditating on them and applying them in my life has brought my family from a place of lack to a place of abundance. What I have listed above is not all that God has to say about money. I encourage you not to stop with what I have shared with you, but consider it a start. Continue to search the Word of God for yourself and apply it to your life and watch God expand you in the arena of finances as He causes men to give into your bosom abundantly.

CHAPTER VI

PREPERATION FOR TRANSITION

Now that you are saved and filled with the Spirit of God you should note that your salvation process has just begun. Many feel that once they are saved that that's all there is to their salvation. That is not true, and if you believe that, you have been deceived by the devil. Your conversion (salvation) is just the beginning of many transitional periods that will take place in your life. In other words, your growth process has just begun.

A spiritual baby needs the milk of the Word of God. It does not matter if you are 80 or 90 years of age, if you have just received Jesus as Lord of your life, you are only a baby in Christ [Spirit].

In this chapter, with the help of the Holy Ghost I am going to show you how to prepare for the transitional periods that you will encounter as a child of God. The Bible tells us that we are transformed by the renewing of our minds by the Word of God, and that we are being changed from glory to glory and from faith to faith. All of this, my friend, represents transition.

And be not conformed to this world: but be ye transformed by the renewing of your mind, that ye may prove what is that good, and acceptable, and perfect, will of God.

-Romans 12:2 (KJV)

But we all, with open face beholding as in a glass the glory of the Lord, are changed into the same image from glory to glory, even as by the Spirit of the LORD.

-II Corinthians 3:18 (KJV)

For therein is the righteousness of God revealed from faith to faith: as it is written, The just shall live by faith.

-Romans 1:17 (KJV)

TYPES OF TRANSITION

Before teaching you how to prepare for the transitions that will be taking place in your life, I want to identify and define a few types (or forms) of transitions.

The first area we will study is in the area of repentance. Webster's Dictionary defines "repentance" as "to feel so contrite over one's sins as to change or decide to change one's ways." The first step that a person will take before receiving his/her salvation is repentance.

Once a person repents he or she has made the transition from death to life. Repentance is the first step a man, woman, boy or girl will take when changing from having a fallen nature to a having a redeemed nature. For without repentance, mankind cannot enter into the kingdom of God.

...let your hearts be turned from sin

-Mark 1:15 (Bas)

And Jesus answering said unto them, they that are hole need not a physician; but they that are sick.

I came not to call the righteous, but sinners to repentance.

-Luke 5:31-32 (KJV)

Repent ye therefore, and be converted, that your sins may be blotted out, when the times of refreshing shall come from the presence of the Lord;

-Acts 3:19 (KJV)

The second area of transition we as Christians should experience is the baptism of the Holy Spirit. Notice I said **should experience.** There are many people in the Body of Christ who have taken the first step (repentance). However, (although) they are saved, they have no power; they are powerless saints. I believe that the baptism of the Holy Ghost is a vital part of Christianity. In fact, I venture to say that if a person is not filled with the Spirit of God, he or she is powerless and has no chance against the devil and his troops. Let me give you a couple of examples.

It was not until Jesus was baptized and the Spirit of God came upon Him that He could walk in the power of the Father and begin to cast out devils, raise the dead, and heal the sick. Up until that time, He was only a man like you and me. It was not until He was endowed with power from on high that He was able to begin to perform miracles.

He became the Anointed Word in the flesh after the Spirit came upon Him. If Jesus had to receive the baptism of the Holy Ghost, what makes the Body of Christ of today any different?

Now when all the people were baptized, it came to Pass, that Jesus also being baptized, and praying, the heaven was opened,

And the Holy Ghost descended in a bodily shape like a dove upon him, and a voice came from heaven, which said, Thou art my beloved Son; in thee I am well pleased.
-Luke 3:21-22 (KJV)

And he arose out of the synagogue, and entered into Simon's house. And Simon's wife's mother was taken with a great fever; and they besought him for her.

And he stood over her, and rebuked the fever; and it left her: and immediately she arose and ministered unto them.
-Luke 4:38-39 (KJV)

Now when he came nigh to the gate of the city, behold, there was a dead man carried out, the only son of his mother, and she was a widow: and much people of the city was with her.

And when the Lord saw her, he had compassion on her, and said unto her, weep not. And he came and touched the bier: and they that bare him stood still. And he said, Young man, I say unto thee, arise. And he that was dead sat up and began to speak. And he delivered him to his mother.

-Luke 7:12-15 (KJV)

The second example I want to give you is taken from the first chapter of the book of Acts. In reading this chapter we find that it was not until the disciples were empowered by the Spirit of God that they received the boldness and power to do the work of Christ after His ascension to the Father. If being filled with the Spirit of God was not an important factor in our lives, then I don't think Jesus would have told His disciples to tarry in Jerusalem until they received the power of God.

And, being assembled together with them, commanded them that they should not depart from Jerusalem, but wait for the promise of the Father, which, saith he, ye have heard of me.

For John truly baptized with water; but ye shall be baptized with the Holy Ghost not many days hence.

When they therefore were come together, they asked of him, saying, Lord, wilt thou at this time restore again the kingdom to Israel?

And he said unto them, It is not for you to know the times or the seasons, which the Father hath put in his own power. But ye shall receive power, after that the Holy Ghost is come upon you: and ye shall be witnesses unto me both in Jerusalem, and in all Judaea, and in Samaria, and unto the uttermost part of the earth.

-Acts 1:4-8 (KJV)

And when they had prayed, the place was shaken where they were assembled together; and they were all filled with the Holy Ghost, and they spake the word of God with boldness.

-Acts 4:31 (KJV)

The infilling of the Holy Ghost is as vital today as it was on the day of Pentecost because for years the Church has lacked boldness and power.

And that's why the devil has nearly taken over. In reading Acts chapter 4 and verse 31 we see that boldness came to the Church as a result of the baptism of the Holy Ghost. If the Church needed boldness and power then, why shouldn't the Church need the power and boldness that is the result of being filled with the Spirit today?

Then certain of the vagabond Jews, exorcists, took upon them to call over them which had evil spirits the name of the Lord Jesus, saying, We adjure you by Jesus whom Paul preacheth.

And there were seven sons of one Sceva, a Jew, and chief of the priests, which did so.

And the evil spirit answered and said, Jesus I know, and Paul I know; but who are ye?

And the man in whom the evil spirit was leaped on them, and overcame them, and prevailed against them, so that they fled out of that house naked and wounded.

-Acts 19:13-16 (KJV)

A closer look at Acts chapter 19 and verses 13–16 is proof that without the power or anointing of God on our life, we won't have a chance against the devil. Notice what the evil spirit said to the seven sons of Sceva after they attempted to cast him out of a person.

The devil said that he knew Jesus and Paul but he did not know them (the seven sons). I believe that the devil knew Jesus and Paul because of the anointing. I believe with all my heart that that devil had an encounter with both Paul and the Anointed One (Jesus Christ). In other words, Jesus and Paul both had the opportunity to cast that devil out of someone at some point. It was because of the anointing that they were able to do the work of the Father.

If you do not have the power, you do not have anything to help you defeat the devil when he rears his ugly head in your life. During your walk with God, you may hear the word "converted" used a number of times. I encourage you not to let the use of the word confuse you. Being converted is just another way of saying are you saved. Webster's Dictionary defines the word "convert" as "to change from one form or use to another."

Dr. Thaddeus M. Williams Sr.

Therefore, being converted means making a transition from one way of life to another.

And said, Verily I say unto you, Except ye be converted, and become as little children, ye shall not enter into the kingdom of heaven.
-Matthew 18:3 (KJV)

And he said unto them, Unto you it is given to know the mystery of the kingdom of God: but unto them that are without, all these things are done in parables:

That seeing they may see, and not perceive; and hearing they may hear, and not understand; lest at any time they should be converted and their sins should be forgiven them.
-Mark 4:11-12 (KJV)

At this point I would like to reaffirm something that I said earlier. Just because a person has repented, gotten filled with the Holy Ghost, and converted does not mean that they have arrived to their final destination. No, as I said earlier that person is a baby in the Lord and their growth process has just begun.

The final area I want to discuss with you is the area of transformation or being transformed. Webster's Dictionary defines the word "transform" as "to change the form, outward appearance, condition, nature, function, personality, or character." With the above definition in mind let's reflect a moment on something I mentioned in a previous chapter. I said that before a person is born again he or she has a fallen nature, and that fallen nature is the result of Adam's disobedience to God in the garden.

However, when the same person receives Jesus as their Lord and Savior, that person takes on the nature and image of God once again. Yes, there is an initial transformation when one accepts Jesus into their heart. But salvation goes beyond that. Even though we are saved, our minds still have to be transformed.

Romans chapter 12 and verse 2 tells us that we are to be transformed by the renewing of our mind by the Word of God. The Amplified Bible puts it this way, "...but be ye transformed (changed) by the [entire] renewal of your mind [by its new ideals and it's new attitude]...." Even though we are born again there is still some transforming that has to take place in our lives because of our old mindsets.

The word transformed used in Romans 12:2 is a very unique word. It is the Greek word "metamorphoa" which is the same word we get our word metamorphosis. Metamorphosis is the physical transformation that different bugs and insects go through before becoming something beautiful. Take a butterfly for example. Prior to its metamorphosis the butterfly is nothing more than a nasty looking worm (caterpillar). It is very slimy and many people don't care to touch or look at it. But after it goes through its metamorphosis, something of beauty emerges and in certain parts of the country and world many people travel from miles around just to see these beautiful creatures.

It is the same with mankind. We must go through a metamorphosis in order to become a thing of beauty to the world. A person may be saved and filled with the Holy Ghost yet have a nasty attitude toward others, and many times they see themselves as something less than what God does. Why? Because of the world's influences. Even though we are saved, there are still a lot of things that you and I (as born-again believers) must allow the Word of God to extract from our minds (souls) in order for us to go from glory to glory.

Prior to my born again experience; I had a very nasty attitude. I was mad at everybody and everything in the world. At times I didn't even like myself. Even after I was saved I still had nasty ways and some issues that had to be dealt with, because they weren't pleasing to God at all. As I began to meditate on the Word, the metamorphosis [transformation] process began and pretty soon those nasty ways and attitudes that I once had no longer existed in my life; and I became a changed man and a thing of beauty to my wife and family.

Today we are starting to see this metamorphosis take place in the Church in a very powerful way. Why? Because the Church has learned to allow the Word of God to have first place, transforming her into a thing of beauty, which draws the world to us in all of our glory.

Arise, shine; for thy light is come, and the glory of the LORD is risen upon thee.

For, behold, the darkness shall cover the earth, and gross darkness the people: but the LORD shall arise upon thee, and his glory shall be seen upon thee.

And the Gentiles shall come to thy light, and kings to the brightness of thy rising.

Lift up thine yes round about, and see: all they gather themselves together, they come to thee: thy sons shall come from far, and thy daughters shall be nursed at thy side.

Then thou shalt see, and flow together, and thine heart shall fear, and be enlarged; because the abundance of the sea shall be converted unto thee, the forces of the Gentiles shall come unto thee.

-Isaiah 60:1-5 (KJV)

PREPARING FOR TRANSITION

Now that you are saved and filled with the Spirit of God, let me give you a few pointers from the Word of God that will help you prepare for what is ahead of you in the area of transition. Keep in mind that transition is a very good thing in God and it is a sign of growth and prosperity. Stay focused and do not let the friction and pressure discourage you from moving ahead in God.

When you start to feel friction or resistance when you make the decision to move with the Lord don't be surprised. The friction you will feel is the result of your moving from one spiritual place to another. That's right, friction occurs because of movement, according to the Law of Statics.

What is Statics? Statics is the branch of mechanics dealing with bodies, masses, or forces at rest or in equilibrium. "Friction" is defined as "a force that resists motion or attempted motion." Therefore, friction is the opposing force that occurs because of movement. It is a symptom that will stop only when a person decides to stop moving in God. But we are not about to stop in God because we are encouraged by the Word of God to press toward the mark of the high calling.

Brethren, I count not myself to have apprehended: but this one thing I do, forgetting those things which are behind, and reaching forth unto those things which are before,

I press toward the mark for the prize of the high calling of God in Christ Jesus.

-Philippians 3:13-14 (KJV)

It is sad, but many Christians today are in the same place they were ten to twenty years ago because they stopped moving with God when the opposing force to spiritual movement was felt in their life. They never realized that the friction they encountered was the result of their making a decision in their heart to believe God no matter what. Because of a lack of knowledge, they fell in their journey with God.

My people are destroyed for lack of knowledge: because thou hast rejected knowledge, I will also reject thee, that thou shalt be no priest to me: seeing thou hast forgotten the law of thy God, I will also forget thy children.

-Hosea 4:6 (KJV)

In other words, they were not prepared for transition, so the friction they experienced caused them to draw back in God. So what should we do to prepare ourselves for transition and to prevent the above from happening to us? I'm glad you asked the question, but before I answer you let me take this time to encourage you to read what I am about to say very carefully. Take the following information and hide it in your heart. Then ask God to bring it to your remembrance whenever you start to feel a little friction after you have decided to yield to the unction of the Holy Spirit.

STEPS IN PREPARING FOR TRANSITION

1. Pray and mediate on the Word of God.

This book of the law shall not depart out of thy mouth; but thou shalt meditate therein day and night, that thou mayest observe to do according to all that iswritten therein: for then thou shalt make thy way prosperous, and then thou shalt have good success.

-Joshua 1:8 (KJV)

Recite it over in your heart.

-Joshua 1:8 (NAB)

2. Put old things behind you.

Brethren, I count not myself to have apprehended: but this one thing I do, forgetting those things which are behind, and reaching forth unto those things which are before,

-Philippians 3:13 (KJV)

That ye put off concerning the former conversation the old man, which is corrupt according to the deceitful lusts;

And be renewed in the spirit of your mind;

And that ye put on the new man, which after God is created in righteousness and true holiness.

-Ephesians 4:22-24 (KJV)

3. Don't fear what is ahead of you.

For God hath not given us the spirit of fear; but of power, and of love, and of a sound mind.

-II Timothy 1:7 (KJV)

4. Be pliable to receive the new wine of God.

And he spake also a parable unto them; No man putteth a piece of a new garment upon an old; if otherwise, then both the new maketh a rent, and the piece that was taken out of the new agreeth not with the old.

And no man putteth new wine into old bottles; else the new wine will burst the bottles, and be spilled, and the bottles shall perish.

But new wine must be put into new bottles; and both are preserved

-Luke 5:36-38 (KJV)

5. Put on the whole armor of God.

Finally, my brethren, be strong in the Lord, and in the power of his might.

Put on the whole armour of God, that ye may be able to stand against the wiles of the devil
-Ephesians 6:10-11 (KJV)

6. Pray in the Holy Ghost to build yourself up in faith.

But ye, beloved, building up yourselves on your most holy faith, praying in the Holy Ghost...
-Jude 20 (KJV)

7. Keep in mind that God will never leave you or forsake you.

Let your conversation be without covetousness; and be content with such things as ye have: for he hath said, I will never leave thee, nor forsake thee
-Hebrews 13:5 (KJV)

8. Remember you have the mind of Christ.

For who hath known the mind of the Lord, that he may instruct him? But we have the mind of Christ.
-I Corinthians 2:16 (KJV)

9. Remember to remain faithful in your call and to your pastor who is the shepherd of your soul.

...For ye were as sheep going astray; but are now returned unto the Shepherd and Bishop of your souls
-I Peter 2:25 (KJV)

10. Remember to continue to press and move forward in God.

I press toward the mark for the prize of the high calling of God in Christ Jesus.

-Philippians 3:14 (KJV)

11. Keep Jesus as your focal point.

Looking unto Jesus the author and finisher of our faith; who for the joy that was set before him endured the cross, despising the shame, and is set down at the right hand of the throne of God.

-Hebrews 12:2 (KJV)

12. Remember never to cast away your confidence in God.

Cast not away therefore your confidence, which hath great recompense of reward.

-Hebrews 10:35 (KJV)

13. Think on pure and holy things.

Finally, brethren, whatsoever things are true, whatsoever things are honest, whatsoever things are just, whatsoever things are pure, whatsoever things are lovely, whatsoever things are of good report; if there be any virtue, and if there be any praise, think on these things.

-Philippians 4:8 (KJV)

14. Cast down evil thoughts.

Casting down imaginations, and every high thing that exalteth itself against the knowledge of God, and bringing into captivity every thought to the obedience of Christ.

-II Corinthians 10:5 (KJV)

15. Remember you can't put new wine in old wineskin.

And he spake also a parable unto them; No man putteth a piece of a new garment upon an old; if otherwise, then both the new maketh a rent, and the piece that was taken out of the new agreeth not with the old.

And no man putteth new wine into old bottles; else the new wine will burst the bottles, and be spilled, and the bottles shall perish.

But new wine must be put into new bottles; and both are preserved.

-Luke 5:36-38 (KJV)

The above steps I have given you are only a sample of what you should do and remember in your walk with God. I encourage you to dig in your Bible and find out what else God would have you to do when making a transition in your life. Staying focused and applying the above to your life will help you and cause you to make the transition God is calling you and many of his people to make in these last days.

CHAPTER VII

TRANSITION IN YOUR PERSONAL LIFE

This chapter is the most important one in this book. It is the one that will help you understand exactly what happens to a person when he or she makes the transition from death to life, from cursing to blessing. I believe that the words contained in this chapter will give you a more clear view of what takes place at the new birth.

I pray that you will take what is written on the next few pages and meditate on it day and night until it becomes real in your heart. I believe that if you do, the Spirit of God will allow revelation knowledge to flow through your inner man and you will never be the same again. Therefore, I encourage you to relax and listen to what the Lord is saying to you through this God-inspired word.

THE BORN AGAIN EXPERIENCE

Jesus answered and said unto him, Verily, verily, I say unto thee, Except a man be born again, he cannot see the kingdom of God.

Jesus answered, Verily, verily, I say unto thee, Except a man be born of water and of the Spirit, he cannot enter into the kingdom of God

-John 3:3 and 5 (KJV)

Since the fall of Adam every human born in this world is born in sin. In other words, when a child is born, it is born separated from God. The life of God is nowhere in his or her nature. This is because when Adam fell, mankind fell with him. Man was separated from his creator and he no longer had dominion in the earth as God had originally planned.

The Bible tells us that man was created in the image of God, but was separated from the presence of God because of sin. When Adam fell, a spiritual transition took place. Man, who was once the image of God, became a dead soul. He no longer lived in the light of his creator, but rather in the darkness of him who deceived him. Mankind made a transition from life to death, from liberty to bondage, and from the place of blessing to being cursed.

And God made the beast of the earth after his kind, and cattle after their kind, and everything that creepeth upon the earth after his kind: and God saw that it was good.

So God created man in his own image, in the image of God created he him; male and female created he them
-Genesis 1:25 and 27 (KJV)

And God set them in the firmament of the heaven to give light upon the earth,
-Genesis 1:17 (KJV)

Unto the woman he said, I will greatly multiply thy Borrow and thy conception; in sorrow thou shalt bring forth children; and thy desire shall be to thy Husband, and he shall rule over thee.

And unto Adam he said, Because thou hast hearkened unto the voice of thy wife, and hast eaten of the tree, of which I commanded thee, saying, Thou shalt not eat of it: cursed is the ground for thy sake; in sorrow shalt thou eat of it all the days of thy life;

Thorns also and thistles shall it bring forth to thee; and thou shalt eat the herb of the field;

In the sweat of thy face shalt thou eat bread, till thou return unto the ground; for out of it wast thou taken: for dust thou art, and unto dust shalt thou return

-Genesis 3:16-19 (KJV)

The Bible says that by *"one man (Adam) sin entered into the world and death by sin"* (Romans 5:12). Because of man's offence the whole human race was separated from God. But mankind no longer has to stay separated from Him. We can be made alive in Christ. God has provided a way for sinful man to come back to Him. That way is through the redemptive work of Jesus Christ. First Corinthians chapter 15 and verses 21–22 puts it this way "…in Adam all die…in Christ shall all be made alive."

But not as the offence, so also is the free gift. For if through the offence of one many be dead, much more the grace of God, and the gift by grace, which is by one man, Jesus Christ, hath abounded unto man

-Romans 5:15 (KJV)

For since by man came death, by man came also the resurrection of the dead.

For as in Adam all die, even so in Christ shall all be made alive.
-I Corinthians 15:21-22 (KJV)

Strong's Concordance defines the word "alive" as "to be given life or to be quickened." Therefore, we may read First Corinthians 15:22 like this "…in Christ shall all be given life." The Goodspeed Translation quotes verse 22 like this "…because of their relation to Christ they will be brought to life again." Therefore, in order for mankind to be made alive he must be born again. So what exactly does it mean to be born again, and what takes place when one becomes born again? To answer this question let's take a look at John chapter 3 and verse 6.

That which is born of the flesh is flesh; and that which is born of the Spirit is spirit

-John 3:6 (KJV)

We should note from verse 6 above that flesh is born of flesh, and spirit is born of spirit. Therefore, the answer to the above question is when a person is born again; his/her spirit is re-born. Once Jesus becomes your

Lord and Savior your spirit is made alive by the Spirit of God. To put it another way, when Jesus comes to live in a person's heart the transition that took place when Adam fell is reversed and that man takes on the image of God once again.

> *The first man is of the earth, earthy; the second man is the Lord from heaven.*
>
> *As is the earthy, such are they also that are earthy: and as is the heavenly, such are they also that are heavenly*
> **-I Corinthians 15:47-48 (KJV)**
>
> *But we all, with open face beholding as in a glass the glory of the Lord, are changed into the same image from glory to glory, even as by the Spirit of the LORD*
> **-II Corinthians 3:18 (KJV)**

Therefore, the first transition a person may encounter in his/her personal life is the born again experience which is the transition from death to life, from lack to abundance, and sickness to health. It is when old things are passed away and all things become new.

> *Therefore if any man be in Christ, he is a new creature: old things are passed away; behold, all things are become new*
> **-II Corinthians 5:17 (KJV)**

FROM POWERLESS TO POWERFUL

There are many Christians in the world today who are powerless in their walk with God. They live defeated lives because they do not know what is available to them as born again Christians. After experiencing the new birth, many people stop searching the scriptures and are unaware of the next step they need to take in order to live a victorious life. However, this is the time to delve into the scriptures to see the promises of God and all that is available to those who serve Him.

Many have been taught from pulpits around the world that the baptism of the Holy Ghost is not for today. Some are afraid to receive the baptism of the Holy Spirit for fear of receiving an unholy spirit. As a result, these saints are not living in the power that God has provided for His Church.

For years these people have been powerless and the devil has used them for punching bags. So what am I saying to you? I am saying that just because a person is saved doesn't mean he has the power of God operating in his life. Even though Jesus was and is the Son of God, He did not have the power of God working in His life until He received the baptism of the Holy Ghost.

> *And Jesus, when he was baptized, went up straightway out of the water: and, lo, the heavens were opened unto him, and he saw the Spirit of God descending like a dove, and lighting upon him:*
> **-Matthews 3:16 (KJV)**

It wasn't until the Holy Ghost came upon Jesus that He could do any miracles. Up until that time He (Jesus) was only a man just like you and me. He was the Word of God that came in the flesh to dwell among men. But the Bible tells us that He emptied himself of all deity before coming to this earth. Jesus did not come to this earth as God. But He lived and ministered as a man anointed by God. Now you may not believe what I am about to say at this point. But if Jesus had not been filled and baptized with the Holy Ghost, He would have never accomplished what He did for you and me when He gave His life on the cross.

> *In the beginning was the Word, and the Word was with God, and the Word was God.*
>
> *In him was life; and the life was the light of men*
> **-John 1:1 and 4 (KJV)**
>
> *...but emptied himself*
> **-Philippians 2:79 (ASV)**
>
> *Let this mind be in you, which was also in Christ Jesus.*
>
> *Who, being in the form of God, thought it not robbery to be equal with God.*
>
> *But made himself of no reputation, and took upon him the form of a servant, and was made in the likeness of men.*

And being found in fashion as a man, he humbled himself, and became obedient unto death, even the death of the cross
-**Philippians 2:5-8 (KJV)**

And he commanded them to be baptized in the name of the Lord. Then prayed they him to tarry certain days
-*Acts 10:38 (KJV)*

If Jesus, the Son of God, had to be filled with the Spirit of God to live a powerful and victorious life, then what makes you and me any different? Think about it for a moment. If Jesus, our Lord and Savior, needed the Holy Ghost in His life, shouldn't we, if we desire to have the power of God manifest in our lives? Therefore, the second transition a person may encounter in his or her life as a believer is the baptism of the Holy Ghost with the evidence of speaking in tongues.

Being Filled With the Holy Ghost

I want to take this time to ask you a few questions if you are a believer.

1. **Has your life been a powerless life?**
2. **Do you see the power of God manifested in your life?**
3. **Are you casting out devils, laying hands on the sick and seeing them recover?**
4. **Do you speak in tongues?**

If your answers to the above questions are no, then you need to be filled with the Holy Ghost. However, you must be born again to receive this baptism of the Holy Ghost. If you are not saved and Spirit-filled and you would like to be, I encourage you to pray the following prayers.

Prayer for Salvation

Heavenly Father, I come to you in the Name of Jesus. Your Word says, *"...whosoever shall call on the name of the Lord shall be saved"* (Acts 2:21). I am calling on you. I pray and ask Jesus to come into my heart and be Lord over my life according to **Romans 10:9-10 that states, "If thou shalt confess with thy mouth the Lord Jesus, and shalt believe in thine heart that God hath raised him from the dead, thou shalt be saved."** I do that now. I confess that Jesus is Lord, and I believe in my heart that God raised Him from the dead. I am now reborn! I am a Christian and a child of Almighty God! I am saved!

Now begin to praise God for your new life in him. Thank him for bringing you out of darkness into his marvelous light. If you have just received Jesus as your Lord and Savior or if you are already saved and desire to receive the baptism of the Holy Ghost then pray the following prayer:

PRAYER FOR THE BAPTISM IN THE HOLY GHOST

Lord you said in Your Word, that *"If ye then, being evil, know how to give good gifts unto your children: how much more shall your heavenly Father give the Holy Spirit to them that ask Him?" (Luke 11:13)* I'm asking You to now fill me with your Holy Spirit. Holy Spirit, rise up within me as I praise God. I fully expect to speak with other tongues as You give me utterance *(Acts 2:4)*.

Now begin to praise God for filling you with His Spirit. Speak those words and syllables you receive not in your own language, but in the language given to you by the Holy Spirit. You have to use your own voice. God will not force you to speak. Now you are a Spirit-filled believer! The Bible tells us to pray in our most holy faith. The more you practice with your new prayer language, the more confidence you will get in it. The Bible also tells us to pray without ceasing. Practice with your new prayer language; you'll never be the same. Since you are now saved and filled with the Spirit of God, expect to see the power of God manifest in your life.

SUMMARY

Transition puts a demand on, and requires a lot of a person. It is a sign of growth and maturity and going from one level to another in the things of God. It is also the way God takes a person from glory to glory in order to bless them in these last days.

As you transition in your walk with God, the winds may blow, the floods may come, obstacles may pop up, and there may be some resistance. But by and through faith you will make it. I encourage you, if you are feeling the pressure of change in your life; stay focused on the Word of God and remain firm in purpose as He molds you into a vessel of gold and honor.

This is the dawning of a new day – the third day, which is the day of perfection. Remember that the road of transition is a wonderful road to travel if understood. However, in order to travel it one must have a strong, yet teachable spirit.

ABOUT THE AUTHOR

D r. Thaddeus M. Williams was born and raised in Birmingham, Alabama. At the early age of ten, God called him to minister His Word. In 1979, Thaddeus graduated from Wenonah High School and entered Tennessee State University where he received a Bachelor of Science Degree in Architectural Engineering. After receiving his degree in 1986, he married his sweetheart, Vinnie Pugh, and moved to Ft. Walton Beach, Florida, where he began his career as a Civil Engineer with the US Army Corps of Engineers.

In 1994, Thaddeus and his wife Vinnie moved to Pensacola, Florida, to attend Bible Training School. He served for more than ten years as an amour bearer and elder; and in July 2000 he and his wife received a promotion from the Lord and began serving as Assistant Pastors for 8 years in their home church. On July 24, 2005, Dr. Williams received his Ph.D. in Theology. He has preached to hundreds of people around the world through the agency of the internet as well ministered to US Troops while serving a one year tour of duty in Baghdad, Iraq with the US Army Corps of Engineers

He is the Founder and President of The Way Ahead Ministries, Pensacola, Florida and has authored five books which will soon be released. Dr. Williams is the father of three wonderful children. He and his wife currently reside in Pensacola, Florida with their children Thaddeus, Jr. – 24; Bryant – 22; and Taryn – 21.

ACKNOWLEDGMENTS

I want to take this opportunity to acknowledge all of my family and friends and thank them for their friendship and love. I especially want to thank three couples that I consider to be my God-sent friends. It is my belief that a person can have friends and then they can have **FRIENDS!** Thanks Lance and Sarah, Brad and Jessica, and Robert and Gloria for being my **FRIENDS!** Vinnie and I value your love and friendship. Thanks for all your prayers and support as you have watched us journey into what God has called us to do. Thanks a million my friends and God bless you **ABUNDANTLY ABOVE ALL THAT YOU CAN ASK OR THINK.**

For more information about The Way Ahead Ministries
Please contact us at:
www.thewayaheadministries.com